A

BOOK OF
DAYS

INTRODUCTION

One of the most familiar scenes at Christmas is of the stable at Bethlehem, whether it be as a crib at home or in church, or perhaps acted out by the children in the local school or church.

St Francis is attributed with the invention of the Christmas crib scene, but every nativity scene assembles a group of characters, some ancient and some modern, which do not necessarily have an obvious similarity to the story of the birth of Jesus as it is told in either of its two versions, in the Gospel according to Matthew and the Gospel according to Luke. Indeed, even these two Gospels offer very different accounts of the birth of Jesus, with different casts, albeit that the presence of the Holy Family remains at the heart of the drama.

Down through the centuries, new characters such as St Nicholas have joined the story and the celebration of Christmas and, in addition, new stories have been told or elaborated about the characters already there.

This book, which draws on the traditions of the medieval books of hours that brought together prayers for the noble patrons who commissioned them, is a Book of Days, numbering the days from the beginning of December until Christmas. This does not entirely match the season of Advent, which is calculated in a different way, but each chapter of this book can be assigned to one day in the month of December, from the 1st to the 25th. The intention is to revisit each of the characters that make up our Christmas story, and to discover what we know about them, and the stories we tell about them.

Each chapter offers an exploration that draws upon the Scriptures, history and legend in respect of the 'character' of the day – one of the people, places or things that have become integral to the Christmas story as it is commonly received. I have augmented this with my own illustrations that I have adapted from some of the most famous works of art depicting the characters of Christmas at different periods of history. This book also aims to provide some spiritual food to nurture readers through the journey of Advent.

There is no absolute reason why these reflections need to be tied to the calendar for December. The twenty-five chapters investigating the Christmas story could be used at other times in taking us on the journey to Bethlehem and offering a meeting with the characters who populate the nativity narrative. It is my hope that these reflections, whenever they are read, will help us to discover new depths in the Christmas story, to deepen our faith, and perhaps even to learn something new or unexpected; because over two thousand years, the story of Christmas has become filled with unexpected delights arising from Scripture, history, legend and faith.

+*Gregory Llanelwy*
Gregory K. Cameron, Bishop of St Asaph

ANNUNCIATION

The story of the birth of Jesus does not start at Christmas, or even with Advent. Instead it begins in the spring of each year – with an announcement. The date of Lady Day, 25 March, is the first day of the year in the old calendar and, for Christians, the Feast of the Annunciation. For obvious reasons, it is exactly nine months before Christmas Day. However, attention focuses on two characters who are central to the Christmas story – we are invited to reflect upon a girl who is to become a mother, Mary, and a creature of the supernatural, the Archangel Gabriel.

I

Luke is the only Gospel to tell us the inside story of the way in which Mary discovered her pregnancy. While Matthew tells the story from Joseph's point of view, Luke tells the story from the point of view of Jesus' mother – indeed, there is an ancient tradition that Luke had actually met Mary, and listened to her memories of Jesus' birth. For Luke, the Archangel Gabriel is sent from God 'in the sixth month' (of another pregnancy, that of Elizabeth) to announce that Mary is to bear Jesus, who will be 'great, and will be called the Son of the Most High' (Luke 1.32ff). Like Matthew, Luke clearly portrays Mary as a virgin at this stage of the story, despite her betrothal to Joseph, so Mary's reaction is one of dismay: 'How can this be?' Reassured of God's direct action to bring these things to pass, Mary makes the boldest of decisions: 'I am the Lord's servant … may it be as you have said' (Luke 1.38).

II

It used to be believed that 25 December was chosen by the early Christians as the date for Christmas because they wished to appropriate the pagan feast day of 'Sol Invictus', the Unconquered Sun. In fact, the evidence is shaky, and the possibility is that the reverse is true and 25 December was chosen as a feast for Sol Invictus in order to compete with the Christian celebration of Christmas, while linking in to the Winter Solstice, the shortest day of the year, which fell a few days earlier, and when, to some minds, night fails to conquer the power of the day, and the days start to grow longer again.

There is every possibility that 25 March was identified as the date for the Annunciation *before* 25 December was chosen for Christmas. To some of the earliest calendrists (those who tried to sort out the mysteries of the earth's and God's calendar), 25 March, a date associated with the spring equinox, was the first day of creation, and therefore a fitting day to mark the conception of the Son of God. Until 1752, every new year was dated from 25 March, and it was traditionally known as 'Lady Day', a term that is still in use in the English legal system as one of the quarter days, when rents were to be paid and debts settled.

III

For many ancient societies it was conception, not birth, that marked the start of a human life. It also marks the beginning of the central mystery of the Christian faith, the Incarnation, when God takes flesh and begins his dwelling among us. Not surprisingly therefore, the Annunciation became a major theme in Christian art, with all manner of angels greeting the Virgin Mary, who was reputed to have been disturbed in the middle of her prayers (which is why she is shown in this picture with her thumb keeping her place in her book).

Today's picture is based on a painting of the Annunciation by two Renaissance artists, Simone Martini and Lippo Memmi, and is housed at the Uffizi Gallery in Florence. I chose this depiction, painted in 1333, because it seems to me that Martini is very clever at catching emotion by physical stance. Gabriel's cloak swirls outwards as he arrives, drops to his knees, and begins his greeting. The Virgin Mary physically seems to draw back in confusion at the angel's greeting, just as Luke describes her: 'much perplexed'. Blue seems to have become a favourite colour for Mary's robes because in iconography blue is the colour of heaven and of the divine. At the Annunciation, Mary is clothed with the overshadowing of the Holy Spirit, while her humanity peeps out in the red of her dress.

IV

The invitation and call of God to Mary to take on the role of mother of Jesus holds a fascination for Christians not only for their central place in the story of Jesus, but also because it speaks to us of vocation – God's call to us and his purpose for our lives. Mary's response, in accepting God's call, with all its challenges, therefore becomes a model of how we should respond when God calls us: 'May it be as you have said' (cf. Luke 1.38).

We, of course, are unlikely to be sent the Archangel Gabriel to make it plain to us what God wants of us, and fortunately there is probably no task for us as difficult as taking on the role of Mother of the Saviour of the World. However, Christians do believe that there will be a path that God wishes us to follow – if not exactly pre-ordained, then at least an invitation to fulfil the gifts and opportunities that he has given to us – and which becomes for us the path to fullness of life.

Let us pause to reflect, and pray this Advent that God will make his will for our lives clearer and plainer – and that he will assist us in giving the same answer as Mary: 'Your will be done.'

Lord of the Ages, who calls us to live into the fullness of life, and to discover our destiny in your will for our lives, help us to learn from the example of Mary who, though troubled by the message of the angel, was still prepared to say 'yes' to your will. Amen.

DAY 2

THE VIRGIN MARY

The woman at the centre of the Christmas story is Mary, chosen by God to be the mother of Jesus. Her story is bound up with the story of her Son, and we encounter her in the Gospels at key moments of Jesus' life: conception, birth, adolescence, first miracle, death, resurrection, ascension and Pentecost. What has Mary to tell us about the path of the disciple?

I

The Bible gives us very little biography for Mary. Luke places her in the context of her family – she has an elderly cousin, Elizabeth – and she has grown up, it appears, in Nazareth in the north of the Holy Land. Mary is a 'young girl' and, given that women in this age were often quickly married after puberty, she may have been in her mid-teens. She is newly betrothed to Joseph when the visit of the angel turns her world upside down.

The angel's greeting to Mary includes a term that is most often translated as 'full of grace', but Luke uses a single marvellously long Greek word whose meaning is more like 'having already received blessing'. Christians believe that to be drawn into a relationship with God is to be blessed, because to know the source of life is to live a fuller life. Is the blessing for Mary a pregnancy that has already begun, or is it a hint that God has been at work in Mary's life for a long time?

II

The ancient world was awash with stories of divine births. Egypt had her Isis and Osiris; Greek myths celebrated the birth of the many heroes, heroines and semi-divine beings, progeny of the gods and goddesses. What is distinctive here is the claim that this divine birth happens in history – even if the chronology is tortuous. Luke is keen to place Jesus' birth in a particular historical context: 'In the reign of Herod', and during 'the first registration of its kind … when Quirinius was governor of Syria' (Luke 2.2), in spite of the fact that the dates don't easily stack up. The Scriptures are very keen to assure readers that Jesus is rooted in history, born of an identifiable woman.

Of Mary herself, we know very little, and virtually nothing outside of Scripture. Jewish writings of the second century make mention of her but, in a polemical age when Christianity was seen as threatening to Judaism, there is nothing positive, although Mary – as Miriam – is also known in the Islamic scriptures.

III

However, if the history of Mary is scant, legend quickly added a whole biography for her. She is depicted as growing up in the precincts of the Temple in Jerusalem, working on spinning and weaving the cloth that hangs as a covering to the Holy of Holies, or which was used for making priestly vestments. Like much legend, the whole thing is highly symbolic – the woman chosen to become an 'ark', carrying the child who is the Son of God, is herself depicted as working on the accoutrements of the house of the Ark of the Old Testament covenant.

The greeting of the angel also formed the basis for further exploration: it became believed that she who was 'full of grace' had been prepared by God's grace to be the mother of Jesus, even to the extent of being preserved from all sin from the moment she was conceived (the Immaculate Conception), and fast-tracked to the destiny of all those who place their faith in Jesus (the Assumption into Heaven). In the Orthodox tradition, Mary has become the 'All Holy', in whom God's work is present in every moment of her life.

Mary has been invented and reinvented in the imagination of theologians down through the centuries (often men) as the perfect woman, meekly accepting God's will, submissive and receptive. Martin Luther, in a famous passage of his writings, meditated on her humility after the angel's salutation: 'Mary', he wrote in the introduction to his Commentary on the

Magnificat, 'conducts herself as before ... she is not puffed up ... but goes about her usual duties, milking the cows, cooking the meals, washing pots and kettles.' There is something charming about this picture of holiness in ordinariness, even if we are also discomforted by Luther's gender stereotyping!

IV

I do not think that Mary was submissive and mild. It takes a special sort of courage to say 'yes' to God when he asks you to take on a vocation that will bring shame down on your head, and require you to challenge all the conventions of the day. Mary will have to face the suspicion of Joseph, and being mother of the Messiah is not seen by the Scriptures as an easy path: suffering and sorrow are predicted: 'you too will be pierced to the heart' is the prophecy given to Mary (Luke 2.34).

We too may find that God's vocation asks tough things of us. The path of life is seldom smooth, and God does not promise his children any special dispensations from the trials of life. In particular, the command to love your neighbour can and should lead us to show love to some unlovely people or situations, and to bring light into dark places requires a high degree of courage and trust in God.

As we reflect on the challenges that may face us in life, let us pause before praying for the courage of Mary and her openness to God's will.

Father of Light and Life, your call may lead us into difficult places, and invite us to courageous action. Help us to take courage from the example of Mary, who was bold in embracing your call, and who was lifted by your grace to open the way for the birth of Jesus and the salvation of the world. Amen.

DAY 3

GABRIEL

The (Arch)angel Gabriel is the other figure in the story of the Annunciation; but who are the angels, and how do they relate to our world?

I

There are very few named angels in the Bible – only two, or three, depending on how you view the 'canon' or list of authorised books of the Bible. Michael (whose name means 'Who is like God?') appears in the Old and New Testaments as a warrior, and as the 'patron saint' of Israel; an angel called Raphael ('It is God who heals') appears in a book called Tobit, which is accepted as Scripture by Catholic and Orthodox traditions, but held to be of doubtful authority by others; and here at the beginning of Luke's Gospel, Gabriel ('God is my strength') is cited, an archangel who again spans both Testaments and is first named as God's messenger in the Old Testament Book of Daniel.

Gabriel is kept busy as a messenger once again at the beginning of Luke's Gospel. It is he who first speaks to Zechariah in chapter 1 of the Gospel and, six months later, he is the one who is sent to tell Mary that she is to be the mother of Jesus.

II

Angels are mysterious beings who in the Greek of the New Testament are literally God's messengers (*angelos* is simply the Greek for messenger). They appear throughout the Bible. Sometimes it seems that their appearance is just like that of other human beings, so that they are only recognised as angels late on in the story, while in other places they are terrible and fantastic creatures, full of wings and eyes and flame.

Our standard picture of an angel, a human being with the mighty wings sprouting from their shoulders, is probably borrowed from classical Greek and Roman civilisation, in which the guardian spirits of particular cities (the word used is the 'genius' of a city), or the personifications of abstract concepts like Victory, were depicted as gracious androgynous human beings equipped with wings.

Angels in the Scriptures were seen as the servants of God in heaven, part of the heavenly host, who could fight on the side of God, as in the Book of Revelation, or in a passage in the Second Book of Kings (chapter 6). Indeed, one of the frequent titles of God in the Bible is as the 'Lord GOD of Hosts'. Angels were frequently intermediaries between God and humanity, and appear in other stories throughout Christian history, such as the story of how the Archangel Michael appears above what comes to be called the Castle of the Angel (Castel Sant'Angelo) at the end of a period of plague in Rome in the time of Pope Gregory the Great.

III

The Bible is actually quite vague about angels, and descriptions vary a great deal. Legend, therefore, quickly filled the gap. By the fifth century, there were whole catalogues of types of angels, the most famous of which was written by an anonymous writer who borrowed the name of Dionysius the Areopagite, a friend of St Paul who appears in the Book of Acts. He argued that there were nine ranks or choirs of angels, adapting an idea from one of the letters ascribed to St Paul (Colossians, chapter 1), where the apostle had listed spiritual powers at work in the world.

Dionysius' hierarchy of nine choirs of angels begins with the Seraphim (the burning ones), whose name is linked to the Hebrew for a serpent, which may have been their original form, but who are described by Isaiah as having six wings and surrounding the throne of God. Then there are the Cherubim, with two pairs of wings, and the faces of animals, maybe even having animal hooves. Two Cherubim protected the Ark of the Covenant according to the Law of Moses in the Bible, and were probably fierce, winged lion-like creatures. In a surprising twist, the fact that there was an Aramaic word, which sounded like 'cherub' but meant a child, later led to a completely different depiction, and the Cherubim became the sweet winged babies we see in much Renaissance art.

There followed a chain of ranks of angels: Thrones, Dominions, Virtues, Powers, and Principalities. Only then, extraordinarily, come the humble archangels such as Gabriel, the errand runner, just above the rank and file of ordinary, everyday angels.

IV

William Blake, the English poet, painter and mystic who lived at the turn of the nineteenth century, and who is most famous for his poem 'Jerusalem', which was later a hymn, offered a vision of creation in which all the wonders of nature were angelic, and conveying a message of glory from the Most High. Angels perhaps remind us that God's presence permeates the whole of creation, and all things speak of God's power and wonder. To this extent, we may be reassured of God's presence in the beauty of creation, and recognise a message from him in the words of a child or in the wisdom of a neighbour. Like so many biblical characters, we may come to realise that an angel has spoken to us after the event.

As we reflect on the presence of God permeating all creation, let us pause and pray for a clearer vision of God in our own lives.

Creator God, who has spoken through angels and prophets down through the years, help us to discern how you are speaking to us today. May we be attuned to the words you speak to us through many channels, that our eyes and our ears may be open to your living word. Amen.

DAY 4

THE HOLY SPIRIT

Hovering behind the interaction between Mary and Gabriel is the presence of the Holy Spirit, that mysterious person of the Holy Trinity at work in the world. Who is the Holy Spirit, and how is the Spirit present among us?

I

In Luke's Gospel, Gabriel speaks to Mary, promising that it is by the power of the Holy Spirit that her child will be conceived. In Matthew's Gospel, Joseph is assured in a dream that the child is simply 'from the Holy Spirit', but the emphasis in both Gospels is that the human Jesus comes into being as a result of the direct intervention of God. This is no normal human birth.

The words of Gabriel in Luke, which speak of the over-shadowing of the Most High, echo the words of Genesis chapter 1 in which it is the Spirit of God that broods over the world and brings it into being: Jesus is God's new creation.

God's Spirit is at work throughout the Bible, inspiring the prophets of the Old Testament or filling its heroes with divine power, so it is not surprising to hear of the Spirit being at work in Jesus' birth, although later in the New Testament the gift of the Spirit becomes more personal, sent from the Father through the Son to be an advocate and guide at work in the lives of all believers.

II

Words used in Hebrew and Greek are given genders, as in French or Spanish. The Hebrew word used for the Spirit in the Old Testament can be understood to be feminine, and is linked with other feminine words associated with God: Glory and Wisdom. The New Testament Greek word for Spirit is neither masculine nor feminine, but neuter. This opened up a debate in Christianity, leading some theologians, such as Irenaeus, to speak of the Holy Spirit as feminine, and even led to the main Church in Constantinople being dedicated to Santa Sophia, the feminine name in Greek for Holy Wisdom. Others felt this was going too far. Jesus uses titles such as Comforter (masculine in the Greek) to describe the Spirit, and speaks of the Holy Spirit as 'he', while most theologians came to equate the figure of Wisdom in the Old Testament with Jesus, the Word of God, rather than with the Holy Spirit.

It is a reminder, however, that in truth God is beyond human nature, and that God is neither male nor female. Even words like 'Father' and 'Son' can only be metaphors for the relationship between the persons of the Holy Trinity, in spite of the fact they are sanctioned by Scripture.

God is always bigger than any description that we give, and 'The wind blows where it wills; you hear the sound of it, but you do not know where it comes from or where it is going' (John 3.8f). The history of the Holy Spirit can only be written through the perception of faith and, for some, it corrects an overly masculine emphasis on God if we see the Spirit as bearing more feminine characteristics, as with wisdom in the Book of Proverbs.

III

It is hard to depict the mysterious nature of the Spirit, but in one biblical passage the Spirit is given physical form – the Spirit descends on Jesus at his baptism in the form of a dove in all four Gospels. Luke specifically says that this was a bodily dove, while in John's Gospel it is John the Baptist who offers an eyewitness testimony.

Artists, like the anonymous 'Master of Cappenberg' in the sixteenth century, whose representation of the Holy Spirit inspired my own drawing, have followed the Bible, and used a dove to symbolise the Holy Spirit throughout the history of Christian art, not only to illustrate the Gospel stories, but on all other occasions when the Spirit needs to be represented. Two saints in particular are shown with the dove of the Holy Spirit – St David, Patron Saint of Wales, where the Spirit in the form of a dove is shown whispering the words he must speak into his ear, and St Gregory, the father of Gregorian Chant, where the dove of the Holy Spirit is seen on his shoulder, whispering music lessons on the composition of the modes of the chant.

In all the legends of the saints, it is the Spirit who inspires and guides them, empowering deeds of strength, words of wisdom, and acts of love.

IV

If the Holy Spirit was important to Jesus' life, bringing about his conception, anointing him at baptism, and driving him out into the wilderness at the start of his ministry, Jesus also speaks of the Spirit as a gift to be conferred by God on every believer. In the Acts of the Apostles, and for the Apostle Paul in his letters, it is the presence and action of the Holy Spirit that authenticates a person as a Christian.

Yet the gift of the Spirit is not one to be given conditionally or on merit; instead, the outpouring of the Spirit is an act of God's grace, his freely given love to the world. Indeed, the Spirit has been described as the love between the Father and the Son, and the Spirit as God's love at work in the world. The Spirit bearing God's love is in fact closer to us than we may dare to believe.

As we pause to reflect, let us think about how God's Spirit may have been at work in our lives, guiding and directing, opening out new possibilities in God's love.

Holy Spirit, gift of God to the world, reveal your presence in our lives by the blessing of your grace, and the comfort of your tender love. Enable us to see where you are at work, and minister in mercy to those for whom our prayers are needed. Amen.

JOSEPH

When the news of Jesus' birth is announced by the angel, Mary is already betrothed to a man called Joseph. If the Gospel according to Luke is the tale of Mary, the Gospel of Matthew appears to tell the story from Joseph's point of view. Today we meet Joseph, called to be a father in a way he could never have anticipated.

I

There is no Gabriel here. Matthew simply records that, before they had become intimate, Mary was 'found to be with child'. Mary's pregnancy, then, is discovered before the betrothed couple had come together, so Joseph quite naturally determines to put Mary aside. He seems a decent sort, seeking to avoid bringing shame upon her, but also a religious man – God is able to speak to Joseph through his dreams. Indeed, Joseph, the father of Jesus, has a lot in common with his Old Testament namesake – both are dreamers and interpreters of dreams.

An early dream reassures Joseph that his son is a gift of the Holy Spirit, destined to be the Saviour, while a later dream warns him to escape the forthcoming wrath and murderous intent of King Herod, and a third informs him of the death of their persecutor. Joseph accepts Mary, and cares for her and her child, taking them to safety in Egypt, and ultimately making a home with them in Nazareth.

II

The picture that I have used for St Joseph is adapted from a fresco by the great Renaissance artist Giotto, who worked in Florence in the late thirteenth and early fourteenth centuries, and who depicts Joseph looking lovingly back to his wife and child, as he leads them on a donkey to exile in Egypt.

Joseph, however, does not play a large part in Jesus' life. Jesus is described as 'the son of the carpenter' in Matthew's Gospel, a detail that awards Joseph a trade, but his significance in Jesus' life appears to be minimal, and when Jesus returns to Nazareth at the beginning of his ministry, he is named as 'the Son of Mary', with his mother's name rather than the usual reference to the father. Joseph himself does not appear, and these facts combine to suggest that he is no longer on the scene – although there is a surprising twist: Jesus is named as having at least four brothers, and an unnamed number of sisters. Otherwise, Joseph's history is unknown to the Scriptures. Matthew does give a distinguished family tree for Joseph, linking him to the Royal House of David, and ultimately to Abraham, and this may suggest a more eminent background, but there can be no certainty. The conversation at the crucifixion between Jesus with Mary and John, the beloved disciple, implies that Mary no longer had her own home and that Joseph had already died.

III

As later theologians reflected on the circumstances of Joseph's life (his early disappearance from the biblical record and the existence of brothers and sisters for Jesus), together with a growing desire to heighten an understanding of Mary's purity and virginity, it became popular to see Joseph as an older man, being encouraged to take Mary as a ward, and in time to take her as a second wife, while himself a widower. A rather strange legend had the Temple authorities determining who should care for Mary by requesting all suitable candidates of the line of David to present their walking staffs at the Temple. Joseph is identified as the future guardian of Mary by the flowering of his staff with lilies, despite being ninety at the time.

Later in the Christian tradition, as the role of a good father was seen as something to be encouraged, Joseph – whose life as a saint was very much in the shadow of his wife – re-emerged as a pattern and example of fatherhood, being depicted in modern icons as a key figure in the icon of the Holy Family. In modern times, when the Catholic Church needed a saint who could harness left-wing thinking and be an inspiration for the labourers and working classes, Joseph was given a new designation by

Pope Pius IX in 1870 as 'St Joseph the Worker' and a second feast day (in addition to 19 March) was chosen. In 1955, this feast was transferred to 1 May, to create an obvious connection with Labour Day or International Workers' Day: a modern example of the Church christianising secular or pagan festivals.

IV

It has long been recognised that although men tend to dominate the leadership of the Church, the pews of churches tend to be filled with women. It is not that there aren't a great many male saints to be role models of male devotion to Jesus, but perhaps Joseph emphasises the softer and kinder side of masculinity: he is defined by his care for his wife and the child who is given to him.

Today, we may recall our own fathers – perhaps, although not always for some, with happy memories – or those we know with responsibility as parents. It is a great responsibility, and as a society we do not offer any training to parents, expecting them to call on their own knowledge and experience of parenting in their own lives, or even from fiction they may have read.

As we reflect on Joseph and the nature of human fatherhood, we can remember moments of good family life, and pause to pray for all those living out a calling to parenthood.

God our Father, who gave St Joseph to your Son to be a father and protector, we pray for all called to be parents that they may be given courage and wisdom, grace and love unbounded, in the care of the children given into their charge. Help them to be good examples, and wise educators in the school of life. Amen.

DAY 6

ST NICHOLAS

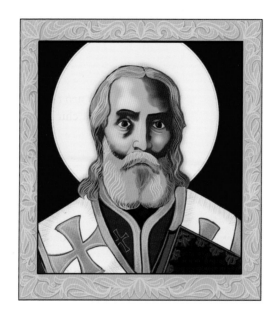

The sixth day of our Advent journey requires a detour, because 6 December has been anciently observed as the feast of a saint with a very intimate modern connection with Christmas – St Nicholas. Who is Nicholas, and how does he relate to the modern Santa?

I

Of course, St Nicholas does not, despite some contemporary misunderstandings, appear in the Bible. The New Testament uses the title 'saint' – which comes originally from the Latin word for 'holy' – to designate all those who have been 'made

21

holy', set apart as belonging to God's Kingdom by being baptised. In the Book of Revelation, the saints of God appear in heaven, where an angel describes them as having 'washed their robes and made them white in the blood of the Lamb' (Rev. 7.14), a reference to Christ's atoning sacrifice on the cross. The title 'saint' began to be used for those whose lives demonstrated especial holiness, in whom the work of God's grace had been especially apparent, which led people to believe that they were certain of being in heaven with the Lord.

II

St Nicholas was the Bishop of Myra in what is today Turkey, but which was then an eastern Province of the Roman Empire shortly after the conversion of the Empire to the Christian faith. Nicholas lived at the end of the third century and the beginning of the fourth, so he personally witnessed the transformation of Christianity from persecuted religion to the state sponsorship that came with the conversion of the Emperor Constantine. These were heady days for the Church, but also difficult ones because there were deep arguments about the true identity of Jesus. One leading Egyptian priest, Arius, argued that Jesus wasn't God incarnate, but a sort of super-exalted angel, and was so persuasive that the global Church began to divide over the issue. Nicholas is said to have been so annoyed by Arius that he swung at him with his fists at one of the Church councils!

It is this (largely overlooked) history of Nicholas as the Middle Eastern Orthodox bishop that I drew on in my picture of the saint, basing my depiction on a portrait imagined by the nineteenth-century Czech painter Jaroslav Mermák.

It is after Nicholas' death, however, that his reputation really takes off. In the medieval period his chief fame was as the patron saint of sailors, and his tomb was at first on the island of Gemile and then at Myra, a centre of pilgrimage – and of pillage. The Italian trading city of Bari sought to make Nicholas their own by kidnapping his bones in 1087, and taking them to their home city to ensure the safety of their fleets. To this day, the city celebrates a feast day in great style on 9 May, the date when St Nicholas' relics traditionally arrived in their new home.

However, there were also legends of Nicholas' special care for children. He is said to have restored to life three children, who had been killed and pickled by a rogue butcher during a time of famine. More particularly, one early story told how he had rescued three poor girls from potential human trafficking, by providing money to be offered as dowries for them, dropping the bags of gold anonymously down the chimney. The seeds of a rapidly growing tradition had been sown.

By the sixteenth century, the cult of St Nicholas had spread from Italy to the Netherlands, and it was here that Sinta Klaas, the gift-bearing bishop, really entered into the Christmas spirit. His generosity was now something from which each child was able to benefit, bringing gifts on his feast day to reward the good, while accompanied by 'Zwarte Piet', a rather racist stereotype of a Spanish moor, who might punish the bad. In eastern Europe, St Nicholas was accompanied by the even more terrifying Krampus, a demonic figure with which parents could terrify their children into adopting good behaviour.

By the time Dutch settlers in the United States had brought traditions from the homeland with them, some of these negative accoutrements had been largely and happily disposed of, although Santa Claus, as he had now become, still kept a record of whether children were deserving of Christmas gifts. A merger with the English tradition of Father Christmas, however, meant that the image of the gift-giving bishop was largely swamped by the semi-pagan midwinter spirit, and his origins virtually forgotten, as the North Pole became his residence, and elvish toymakers became his companions.

IV

There are two aspects of Nicholas' story that resonate with the Christian disciple down through the ages. First is his defence of orthodoxy, the right worship, of God to which all Christians are enjoined. The Creed of the Council of Nicaea, which Nicholas attended in AD 325, remains to this day the clearest articulation of fundamental truths defended as the Christian faith 'delivered to the saints'.

However, the second must be his generosity, and the inspiration of his gift-giving at Christmas. We are all called to generosity (2 Cor. 9.6–8), and this reflects the grace of God, who freely gives to us in Christ. 'You received without cost; give without charge' says the Lord (Matt. 10.8). The true worship of God must lead to truly transformed lives.

As we reflect on the generosity and merriment in good things exhibited in the story of St Nicholas, Santa Claus, pause to pray that his spirit may be part of the discipleship we live.

Generous God, you gave us an example of fidelity and generosity in the ministry and example of St Nicholas. In this holy season, may that same example inspire and guide our planning and our actions, our worship and our hopes, so that with him we may follow Jesus, the Lord and Saviour in whose name we pray. Amen.

NAZARETH

Nazareth is the first of two locations for the story leading up to Jesus' birth. The more famous is Bethlehem, but the place from which Jesus is remembered as coming, and the setting for the early parts of the story leading to Jesus' birth, belong to a Galilean backwater called Nazareth. What do we know of the place from which Jesus took his name?

I

Matthew, Mark and John ignore Nazareth almost entirely as the location for the story of Jesus' origins, although all the Gospels acknowledge Nazareth as the place of the eventual home of the Holy Family. The town is, however, at the heart of the opening narrative in Luke as the location to which Gabriel is sent, and the home from which Mary and Joseph must make the long journey to Bethlehem in order to answer the summons of Augustus Caesar to be registered in a census. For Luke, though, Nazareth is always Jesus' true home, and twice he records the Holy Family returning 'to their own home' in Nazareth after later trips to Jerusalem.

II

Nazareth is situated about 64 miles north of Jerusalem so it was a lengthy trek, but even in its heyday the town was considered of little significance. One of Jesus' future disciples even quipped 'Can anything good come out of Nazareth?' so poor was its reputation. Nevertheless, it was the place with which Jesus became inextricably linked, being called 'Jesus of Nazareth', as testified by the titulus, or description and charge, that Pontius Pilate caused to be attached to the cross, as well as other references, while the earliest name for Jesus' disciples was, like their master, 'the Nazarenes'.

Nazareth remained a neglected city throughout its history apart from a brief period under the Crusader kings, who recognised the importance of the site and identified a cave as the site of the Annunciation, building a large church over it. After the reconquest by local Muslim rulers, the site returned to its earlier neglect, and it was only in the twentieth century that a large basilica was built to mark the believed site of the Annunciation by the Catholic Church. The modern Basilica of the Annunciation is built over the cave earlier identified as the place where Mary encountered the angel, and was dedicated in 1969.

III

The fact that Jesus' hometown was such a backwater has added to the sense that Jesus' family came from a poor background. The picture I have created to represent Nazareth is based upon a mosaic of the early fourteenth century which decorates the beautiful but tiny Church of the Holy Saviour in Chora on the outskirts of Istanbul. Nazareth is shown as a typical walled town of the day, humble and without any major structures, and forms part of a cycle of mosaics depicting the Christmas story.

Legend actually identified two sites in Nazareth for the Annunciation and, in addition to the cave, a well is also identified as the place where Mary was reported to have received the angel while drawing water. Interestingly, an early apocryphal (doubtful or rejected) gospel, called the Gospel of James, and which dates to the second century, seems to know both traditions, and reconciles them by recording that Mary first heard the voice of the angel at the well, but it was only when she returned home that Gabriel fully revealed himself. What interests me about this is that, although the Gospel of James is far too late and full of the miraculous to be received as one of the authoritative Gospels, it is very early evidence that the sites later revered as the authentic sites for biblical events in Nazareth are attested from a very early period.

The home of the Holy Family has a strange after-life. This dwelling in Nazareth became the centre of two miraculous stories in the Middle Ages. In 1061 an English noblewoman, Richeldis de Faverches, received a vision and instruction from God to build a replica of the Holy House at Walsingham in England. 'England's Nazareth' went on to establish itself as a major pilgrimage centre, notably resurrecting itself in the nineteenth century after destruction during the Reformation. Even more remarkably, it is reported that the Holy House itself became a 'mobile home', and was carried by angels from place to place in the thirteenth century, before finally coming to rest at Loreto in Italy, where a major shrine exists to this day.

IV

The fact that Jesus came from Nazareth is evidence that God is drawn to the humble and the marginalised. The odd status of Galilee and its towns in the eyes of the people of Judaea affected people's opinion of Jesus later in his life, wondering whether he really could be the Messiah, yet Nazareth becomes the hometown of the Son of God.

It is a reminder to us that God works through the humble, and that he is not only to be found in the awe-inspiring places – in the mountains and the sacred sites embued with history and significance. It is the same with people, and Paul reminds the early Christians at Corinth that 'Few of you are wise by any human standard, few powerful or of noble birth' (1 Cor. 1.26). Jesus himself will choose his disciples from among the fisherfolk and tax collectors.

It is a timely reminder that we do not qualify as children of God because of our talents, or our beauty, or our qualifications. God loves us because we are, and not because of who we are, where we come from, or what we have achieved. Love comes first. Let us pause to reflect on the very ordinariness of the place that Jesus elects to call home. How does God inhabit the things that are ordinary in our own lives?

Lord Jesus, you were content to have Nazareth as your home. Help us to be at peace in our circumstances, not overawed by the talents or possessions of others. You love us for who we are, and our dignity lies in our status as your children. Let us never despise the people or things that are humble, but seek to see your blessing in all. Amen.

DAY 8
JOHN THE BAPTIST

The Gospel according to Luke begins not with the story of the birth of Jesus, but with the story of the birth of a close relative, John the Baptist. John is an important figure in his own right, and understood in Christianity as 'The Forerunner', the one who prepares the way for the Messiah. Who is the Baptist, and what is his vocation?

I

The story of John's birth, which opens Luke's Gospel, is seen – like Jesus' own story – as involving God's intervention. Zechariah, a priest in the Temple, and his wife Elizabeth are unable to conceive, but God grants her a pregnancy in old age. From the beginning, John's role is marked out and defined: 'From his very birth he will be filled with the Holy Spirit; and he will bring back many Israelites to the Lord their God. He will go before him as forerunner …' (Luke 1.15–17). All four Gospels introduce the ministry of Jesus with the preaching of John the Baptist, so named because he baptised his followers. They also all define who John is in the same way, introducing him as a radical teacher and preacher. The Scripture harks back to Isaiah: 'I am a voice crying in the wilderness, Make straight the way for the Lord' (John 1.23).

II

John is described in a way that makes it clear that he stands in the prophetic tradition of the Old Testament: he wears camel skin, and eats locusts (some have suggested locust figs, and not the actual insect!) and wild honey. He lives in the eccentric mould of one of God's prophets, deep in the wilderness, which in the Bible is the place, devoid of other life, to which anyone might go to encounter the stark reality of God's existence.

My picture of John is based on an icon painted by probably the most famous of iconographers, Andrei Rublev, a Russian artist who lived in the sixteenth century, whose own holiness and ability to bring life to the biblical characters is so profound that he himself has been recognised as a saint. Rublev's icon captures the wild nature of John the Baptist, and even what look suspiciously like the dreadlocks of a Rastafarian.

Many scholars have seen links between the style of John the Baptist's ministry and his themes of repentance and God's forthcoming judgement, and the teaching of a community called the Essenes. They were described by the Jewish historian Josephus as a group of Jewish radical believers, who also lived around this time in the Judaean desert. Very little was known about them until the 1940s, when a series of spectacular discoveries, initiated by a shepherd boy, uncovered documents which are today known as the Dead Sea Scrolls. In addition to many of the books of the Old Testament and Hebrew Scriptures, there are also scrolls that speak of the coming of a Messiah of Light, who will bring the judgement of God and cleanse the world. It would be fair to say, though, that while both John the Baptist and the Essenes give a taste of the fervent hopes that existed around these times, no definite links can be proved.

There may even have been some dispute about who exactly *was* the Messiah. The Gospels are at pains to point out that Jesus, not John, is the true Messiah: 'He [John] was not himself the light; he came to bear witness to the light' (John 1.8). At least one early Church leader, Apollos, described in the Book of Acts, knew only of the baptism of John (Acts 18.25), and had to be taught the Christian gospel more clearly. Herod Antipas, the son of Herod the Great, who was responsible for John's eventual death, even thought that Jesus was John come back from the dead.

To this day, there is a small tribal group in Iran and Iraq, called the Mandaeans, who argue that John is the greatest prophet of God, following in the line of Adam, Enoch and Noah among others. Their faith has many similarities with the faith proclaimed in the Dead Sea Scrolls in which the Children of Light are gathered by God to fight against the powers of darkness, although again no historical links have been proved.

III

In legend, John becomes for Christians the bridge figure between the Old and New Testaments. His style and manner of preaching is rooted in the prophetic voices of Elijah and Isaiah and, like them, he challenges the morality of kings and urges people to repent and live a life of justice. Yet he is also a companion of Jesus, recognising him as the true Messiah of Israel, and counting himself among his followers. As the one who prepared the people of Israel for the ministry of Jesus, John has come to be seen as one of the most significant of Jesus' followers, and is often shown on the right hand of the enthroned Christ (with the Virgin Mary on the left) on the iconostasis – which is the wall of icons erected in front of the sanctuary in Orthodox churches.

By a curious twist of symbolism, because the Scriptures refer to John as sent by God to be the messenger to prepare a way for God ('I am about to send my messenger to clear a path before me', Mal. 3.1), and the Greek word for messenger is *angelos*, which was used in the Greek (or Septuagint) translation of these words, John the Baptist is sometimes shown in icons as having the wings of an angel flowing from his shoulders.

IV

John the Baptist called people to be baptised in order to wash away their sins and prepare to receive the Messiah. Baptism was symbolic of the radical cleansing that had to be undertaken in order to enter the Kingdom of God. Ultimately, though, he pointed away from himself towards Jesus. 'He must grow greater; I must become less' he is recorded as saying in the Gospel according to John (John 3.30).

Down through the years, those who seek to be disciples of Jesus can be profoundly grateful for the people, friends, ministers and colleagues who have pointed them in the direction of Jesus, and helped them to see him at work in their lives. Sometimes we need others who can help us to see what God is saying to us, and where he is calling us, while, like those who listened to John's preaching, we can recognise our need to repent – to reset our discipleship and quest for holiness by beginning again.

Pause to reflect on this extraordinary character who prepared the way, and pointed to his Lord. Let us thank God for all those who have helped our journey of faith.

Lord of the World, as we recall the ministry of John the Baptist, who pointed away from himself towards Jesus, we give thanks for all those in our own lives who have revealed Jesus to us. Help us to heed the voices that call us back to faithfulness in our discipleship, and to come to you in repentance and faith. Amen.

ZECHARIAH

Strangely, we know more about the parents of John the Baptist than we do about the parents of Jesus. Who was John's father, and what do the Scriptures tell us about him?

I

Zechariah shares his name with the Old Testament prophet and was a priest serving in the Jerusalem Temple. Luke tells us that as a priest of 'the division of the priesthood called after Abijah' (Luke 1.5), Zechariah had to take his turn in leading the worship of the people, and offering sacrifices on their behalf. It is while he is on duty and entering the Holy Place that Gabriel comes to inform him that his prayer has been heard: his wife, Elizabeth, is to have a child. Because of their age, Zechariah exhibits disbelief, and is rebuked by being struck dumb (which may have given rise to the popular saying about being struck dumb when hearing amazing or surprising news).

Even when John is born, and has been brought to the ceremony of his circumcision, Zechariah has to signify the name he wants for his son in writing. Only then is his tongue released.

II

Revered by generations of Jewish and Christian scholars as one of the greatest buildings ever erected, the Temple of Solomon at Jerusalem was the centre of the worship of the God of Israel. The Bible records it as the only place where God was to be worshipped by blood sacrifice, and the Books of Moses (the Jewish Torah and the first five books of the Christian Old Testament) laid down specific rules for the daily rituals and sacrifices to be observed. Zechariah therefore belongs to a particular historical setting, and is described as being among the elite who served in the Temple.

By the time of Jesus, this was the Second Temple – not the Temple built by Solomon, which had been destroyed by the invading Babylonians six centuries before. A second temple had been established by the Jews when they had been released from exile and captivity by the Persian liberator Cyrus the Great, about seventy years later, but the temple built during the time of the Return, as it was called, had caused much disappointment by the meagreness of its design and its lack of splendour.

It had taken the resources of Herod the Great to restore and enhance the magnificence of the Temple in Jerusalem, in a building programme lasting from 25 BC onwards. Jesus, in his ministry, was confronted by those who objected to his comments about the possible destruction of this Temple: 'It has taken forty-six years to build this temple' said his opponents, not grasping the point of Jesus' teaching. 'Are you going to raise it up again in three days?' (John 2.20).

III

My picture of Zechariah is adapted from a scene painted by the Renaissance artist Domenico Ghirlandaio, at the very end of the fifteenth century, in a great cycle of frescos that he painted of the life of John the Baptist in a chapel of the Church of Santa Maria Novella in Florence. It depicts the scene of the circumcision and naming ceremony in the Temple for John the Baptist. Zechariah is shown as an old man – in line with the suggestion of the Scriptures – and writing down his son's name for the attention of his family who had gathered for his naming.

Moments later, Luke tells us, Zechariah's tongue was freed, and he breaks out in song, singing one of three great songs, or canticles, that are recorded by the evangelist Luke in the birth story of Jesus, and which have formed the backbone of the daily cycle of prayers (the Office) ever since. Called the Benedictus, after its opening word in Latin, Zechariah's canticle is a great hymn of praise of all God's promises, and sets out John the Baptist's destiny to go ahead of the Lord. The Benedictus has become the central element in the Church's celebration of morning prayer, emphasising all that is to come, and the promise of God that his love and compassion will break upon his people like the dawn. It is thus a fitting prayer for the morning, and is complemented by the Song of Simeon, the Nunc Dimittis, which speaks of God's light shining in the world, and which closes the day at Compline, the last service of the day.

IV

Sometimes we will be struck dumb by stories of faith or of the miraculous which we are told, not knowing what to make of them. However, sometimes it is good to admit that we don't know everything, and that we don't have all the answers. At times like this, we would be wise to recall the faith of Zechariah, released from his doubt, who recalls God's promises and the way in which they would be brought to pass.

Even though we don't know the future, and may be dismayed by the challenges before us, we can put our faith in God and, like Zechariah and John, be ready to play our part in bringing the promise of God's enlightening love into every situation.

Let us pause to reflect on the things that have puzzled us in our discipleship, and ask for the eyes of faith to enhance our journey of faith.

Blessed are you, Lord God of Israel. As you inspired Zechariah to pray in delight at perceiving your work in the world and in the birth of his son, help us to praise you in every circumstance of life, and to trust that the promise of your love means that you are with us in every situation. Amen.

DAY 10

ELIZABETH

The mother of John the Baptist is Elizabeth, who plays an important role in supporting the newly pregnant Mary. Who is she, and what role does she play?

I

Luke records that Elizabeth is a member of the priestly house of Aaron, and therefore appropriately married to Zechariah, also of a priestly family. However, she is also a relative of Mary, although the exact relationship is not spelled out. Luke says only that she was a kinswoman, without giving the relationship. As we discovered, Zechariah and Elizabeth had not been able to have children, until in old age Gabriel announced the promise of the birth of a son who would become John the Baptist. Elizabeth appears to have been more trusting than her husband, but withdrew into seclusion throughout her pregnancy, giving thanks for the quiet work of God's grace for her and for her husband.

Gabriel reveals Elizabeth's pregnancy to Mary as a sign that God's promises are to be trusted and will be fulfilled. Perhaps we may be permitted to believe that God enables these two relatives to be a comfort and support to each other in unexpected motherhood.

At any rate, Mary hurries off to visit Elizabeth, and as they meet something remarkable happens: the baby in Elizabeth's womb stirs (Elizabeth later says that he 'leapt for joy') on the approach of Mary; and Elizabeth, aided by the Holy Spirit, discerns the truth: 'Who am I,' she says, 'that the mother of my Lord should visit me?' (Luke 1.43).

The theme of the early chapters of Luke's Gospel, repeated and repeated by Luke, is that God is faithful and keeps his promises – to Zechariah, to Elizabeth, to Mary, to the people of Israel themselves. These stories of faithfulness reinforce one another: as God has been faithful in providing for one, so he will provide for the other.

Mary's response to Elizabeth's greeting is to recite another of the great canticles of Luke's Gospel, known to us from its Latin first word as the Magnificat. She praises the God who keeps his promises, raising up the lowly, and filling the hungry, while the powerful and the rich must fend for themselves.

II

The Feast of the Visitation, celebrated on various days in both the Eastern and Western Churches, became a prominent feast day in the late medieval period. It seems to have been particularly popular among the Franciscans, who promoted its celebration, originally on 2 July, shortly after the Octave of the Feast of the Nativity of St John. I have modelled today's picture on a representation of the Visitation by Piero di Cosimo, a late fifteenth-century artist, and it is noticeable that while Mary is clothed in the familiar blue and red robes associated with her, Elizabeth is portrayed in robes resembling the robes worn by the Poor Clares, also known as the Order of St Clare, or the Second Order of St Francis, which was founded by St Clare, one of the earliest followers of St Francis, and that adopted the strict poverty commended by Francis to his disciples.

III

Elizabeth is not known to history outside of sacred writing, although her life follows a pattern much beloved in the Scriptures – that of the mature woman who has been unable to bear a child until blessed by God in old age. In this respect, she follows in the footsteps of Sarah, wife of Abraham, and Hannah, the mother of Samuel. Children are seen as a sign of God's blessing in the Scriptures, and their lack as a great sorrow, so that part of the outworking of God's love and justice in the world is to balance fate by bringing the blessing of children to those who, in old age, may have believed themselves bereft, at a time when other families have reached their full complement of offspring.

The story of Elizabeth and Mary inspired many retellings, including in the apocryphal gospels, such as the Gospel of

James, not least because it allowed stories to be told of the period of the childhood of Jesus, something that the Gospels in the Bible omit. Greater and greater detail was offered in these apocryphal gospels about the relationship between the two women, and the stories of the birth of their children, so that there is a sort of parallel between them: John and Jesus belong in the same story from the time of their birth, and their destinies are inextricably linked.

IV

The story of the obvious love and compassion between these two women may cause us to think of the rewards of links in our wider families, but it also reminds us that great comfort and strength can be derived from finding fellowship with those who are walking the same path in life – whether joyful or sorrowful. There is a sense in which God does not wish to leave us abandoned and lonely in the story of our lives, and we can look for, and be ready to offer, hospitality with those who share our experiences.

Let us recall those who have walked with us in particular phases of our lives, especially those in our own families, and let us pray that God will help us to use the lessons we have learned in life to assist and support those whom we encounter.

Lord God, who enabled Elizabeth and Mary to recognise in one another the work of your faithfulness, give us companions in our journey through life, who may encourage us, and whom we may encourage, for in the giving and receiving of life, friendship and mercy there are reflections of your own goodness. Amen.

JOACHIM & ANNA

Down through the ages, Christians became very attached to the story of the birth of Jesus, and devotion particularly focused on his Mother, who was accorded the title Our Lady, as Jesus is Our Lord. Not surprisingly, a whole biography developed for Mary, whose parents were named as Joachim and Anna.

I

The Bible probably tells us virtually nothing of Mary's family – I write 'probably' because there are two family trees given for Jesus; one in Matthew's Gospel and one in Luke's. Both of these are most easily understood as the descent in the father's line, but they are different, and some scholars have suggested that this might actually be because the one line of descent is through Mary. If this is the case, then Jesus is 'the Son of David' both through his father and his mother. Luke certainly names Joseph as being 'of the House of David'.

II & III

History and legend are so intertwined here that all we have to speak of is the history of the legend. Mary, of course, will have had a father and a mother, but their names are a matter of mystery. Names seem to have been assigned early on, however, and the first references to Joachim and Anna appear in the apocryphal gospels of the second century. Joachim is said to have come from Nazareth, while Anna had been born in Bethlehem, nicely tying together the two locations that appear in the stories telling the events leading up to Jesus' birth.

By the thirteenth century, these legends were elaborated and codified in a book known as *The Golden Legend*, which gathered together not just the stories associated with Joachim and Anna, but also those of many other saints and martyrs. By then the story of Joachim and Anna had become a much loved narrative in which the elderly Joachim and Anna (where have we seen this pattern before?) both lament that they have not been blessed with a child. Joachim resorts to prayer and fasting in the desert, while Anna is left bereft at home in Jerusalem. Both are vouchsafed a vision by God in which they are told that they will be blessed by a child, whereupon Joachim rushes to be reunited with Anna in Jerusalem, while Anna rushes out to look for him. They meet in a joyful embrace at the Golden Gate, anciently the main entrance of the city, their kiss either speaking of a happy reunion, or mystically representing the moment of Mary's conception.

This happy scene, of an elderly couple rejoicing with each other in the good news given to them by God, became a favourite for depiction in the medieval period, associated with the Feast of the Conception of the Virgin Mary, which was celebrated first in the East, and then in the West, on 8 December, nine months before a feast day for Mary's nativity. The picture I have drawn for today is adapted from a fifteenth-century representation by an anonymous artist known as 'the Master of the Bamberg altarpiece', Bamberg being a German city near Nuremburg. Indeed, the meeting of Anna and Joachim at the Golden Gate became a stock image in a cycle of paintings, of which many examples survive, that detail the life of the Virgin Mary, until the time when such legendary paintings fell out of favour at the seventeenth-century Council of Trent.

As the centuries passed, theologians debated the sinless nature of Jesus, and the need to offer explanations for his perfection arose. He was, said the writer to the Hebrews, 'tempted in every way as we are, yet only without sinning' (Heb. 4.15), but was that merely because Jesus did no wrong, or because he was without the predisposition to sin that the Apostle Paul had argued we inherited from Adam? It was suggested that God's work of redemption must have begun at the earliest point in Mary's life, preparing her for her destiny as the mother of Jesus, in order to ensure that Jesus knew no taint of sin from the beginning. In the Eastern tradition, Mary has been hailed as 'the all holy', because of this presumed attribute granted by God: the mother is redeemed by her son even before he is conceived. In the West, this became the doctrine of the Immaculate Conception – Joachim and Anna had conceived Mary in innocence. Perhaps the kiss had achieved Mary's conception after all.

IV

What permeates the story of Joachim and Anna, however, is their love for each other. Faithful to each other and to God, they seek the blessing of parenthood, but it is in some way a shared task. Informed of God's gracious act, they both rush to inform the other, meeting in that happy embrace at the Golden Gate.

As Christians, we can celebrate the long-term commitment where marriages are successful, or where two people find companionship for life. Love changes down through the years, and although the river at its mouth exhibits little of the bubbling crystal streams associated with its springs, it is a far, far stronger flow. Let us thank God for those who have been a source of stability in our lives, and who have shown us support.

We pause to reflect on love's many facets, thanking God for the joy Joachim and Anna found in each other.

God, the source of all true love, we thank you for those who are nourished and sustained by love, and especially those who have nurtured us. Enable us by the grace of your love, and teach us how to sustain the gift of love in our own relationships, until we come at last to you, both source and summit of human desire. Amen.

DAVID

Another of the characters in the background of the Christmas story is King David, the second King of Israel, and founder of Judah's royal house. But why is this Old Testament figure part of the story of Christmas, and what does he teach us about Jesus?

I

In the greeting of the angel, the name of King David is invoked in connection with the birth of Jesus. Jesus is to be seen as the heir of David. The very first verse of Matthew's Gospel names Jesus as 'the son of David', and Herod is later depicted as suspicious and in fear of a royal rival. In Luke's Gospel, Gabriel specifically says of Jesus: 'The Lord God will give him the throne of his ancestor David' (Luke 1.32), while Zechariah, in the Benedictus, refers to God's acts in fulfilment of the promises he made to David.

One of the enigmas surrounding Jesus is the way in which he linked to Old Testament prophecy. The Scriptures had long described the promised Messiah as a 'Son of David', a King to rival the first David, who was seen as the epitome of godly kingship. It wasn't easy, though, for the earliest Christians to demonstrate a royal background for Jesus from humble Nazareth, and we have noted how two family trees – one in Matthew and one in Luke – were produced as evidence.

II

David's story as told in the Bible dominates the two Books of Samuel, the opening of the First Book of Kings, and the First Book of Chronicles. They tell a clear enough story: David is the son of Jesse of Bethlehem, growing up to be little more than a shepherd boy until the mighty judge and prophet Samuel identifies him as God's chosen successor to the failed first King of Israel, Saul. David begins a long journey to power. He befriends Saul's son, Jonathan, but falls foul of the father, and is exiled to lead the life of a bandit for many years. On the death of Saul and Jonathan at the battle of Gilboa, David is left to lead the defence of the nation of Israel against the Philistines, and he conquers in God's name. It is David who captures the city of Jerusalem from the Jebusites and founds a royal dynasty which has God's seal of approval.

The historical evidence for David outside the pages of Scripture is a little more difficult to pin down, as very little remains by way of archaeological evidence for David or for David's kingdom. However, there are three ancient inscriptions that appear to refer to 'the House of David', but the existence of a strong and united kingdom that ruled over Israel and Judah is still only evidenced in the Bible, and not in the findings of any archaeology to date.

III

In complete contrast to this, legend has seen David as the perfect godly king, even though in the Bible several stories reveal his fallibility. His warrior career and record outshone all that might have besmirched his name, however, and in the eyes of the medieval chroniclers he was the perfect example of chivalry, particularly in his defeat of the giant Philistine warrior Goliath, while he was still a boy. David joined the list of the Nine Worthies, the nine greatest warrior heroes of chivalry for the medievals – Hector of Troy, Alexander the Great, and Julius Caesar; Joshua, David and Judas Maccabeus; Arthur, Charlemagne, and Godfrey of Bouillon, the first Crusader King of Jerusalem.

Not only that, but his reputation as a musician added further lustre to David's name. The fact that so many of the psalms in the Bible are attributed to David meant that he gained a great reputation as a musician. He is often depicted playing his harp, a role remembered to this day when, appearing as the King of Spades in the French deck of cards, David carries his harp for all eternity.

The picture of David accompanying today's reflection is based upon a portrait by Pedro Berruguete, a Spanish artist who painted many 'portraits' of David in the late fifteenth century. Berruguete enjoyed depicting David as an oriental monarch complete with turban and rich jewels. His portraits were received with delight in the courts of Europe, reminding kings of their duty to aspire to be like David.

IV

David is therefore presented as the role model for Jesus, the righteous king who is the object of God's favour and promise. Important as these promises are, however, the Bible speaks of God's eternal horizons as being far greater than human comprehension: 'Where were you when I laid the earth's foundation?' God asks in the Book of Job (Job 38.4). '... in the Lord's sight a thousand years are like one day' wrote the apostle Peter (2 Peter 3.8). In this context, the plan by which God chooses the nation of the Jews to be God's people, and which promises them a ruler like David, who will rule for eternity, is just one element of the wider sweep of salvation history, in which God works out the redemption of all creation.

Christians therefore see God working throughout history to bring forth the goal of a redeemed and holy humanity: all creation waits for the revealing of the sons of God, as the Letter to the Romans puts it (Rom. 8.19). Earthy kingship becomes just a pale reflection of the Kingship of God, and of the Lord Jesus who, as the Son of David, inherits the mantle of all God's plans for salvation.

Let us pause to reflect on the eternal workings of God's providence and plans for humanity, and God's faithfulness to his promises.

God of our ancestors, down through the centuries, you choose a people of your own desire to prepare the way of salvation for the whole of creation. As we remember David, who was your chosen instrument in establishing the people of Israel, help us to see the way in which Jesus is established as the Lord of Creation. Amen.

DAY 13

ST LUCY

The date of 13 December is another feast day for a saint connected with Christmas, but not part of the scriptural story – Lucy. Who is Lucy, and what is her role in the Christmas story?

I

Like Nicholas, Lucy does not appear in the Bible, but because her feast day is so close to Christmas she has got caught up in the Christmas story. The Bible, however, does bear witness to the fact that to be a follower of Jesus is to be open to the possibility of persecution, and to becoming a 'martyr': 'Blessed are you, when you suffer insults and persecution and calumnies of every kind for my sake', said Jesus knowingly (Matt. 5.11). The Greek word 'martyr' merely means a 'witness', but the Bible speaks of being a witness to Jesus as potentially being prepared to die: 'Be faithful till death, and I will give you the crown of life' Jesus is recorded as saying in the Book of Revelation (2.10) and, very soon, the first martyr's death is recorded in the Book of Acts. Stephen is stoned to death after he gives his testimony to Jesus as the Messiah. An early Christian writer, Tertullian, recorded that 'the blood of the martyrs is the seed of the Church', and many have followed in the path that Stephen first trod.

II

Lucy is recorded as a martyr in the last great persecution by the Roman emperors before the conversion of Constantine. She was martyred at Syracuse, having been accused of being a Christian by a jilted suitor. She was said to be from a wealthy family, and has been remembered as one of the foremost martyrs of the early Church.

We do not know the ethnic background of Lucy, but I have chosen here to portray her as of African heritage, drawing on an anonymous portrait of the sixteenth century by the great Italian artist Paolo Veronese. Too often Christian art draws on its European heritage, forgetting that Christ himself was a Middle Eastern Jew, and that disciples of Jesus have been drawn from all nations. However, ancient Rome was much more ethnically diverse than is often credited – at least one line of emperors were African, and it is entirely possible that Lucy herself came from an African family.

III

Like many of the accounts of martyrdom from the earliest years of Christianity, the account of Lucy's martyr's death glories in the violent. The saints, it appears, did not give up their lives quickly, even though they demonstrated great fortitude. Lucy is reputed to have been blinded (which is why she is the patron saint of the blind) before various attempts to put her to death by fire, but finally being stabbed in the neck.

Such accounts are rather gruesome to modern readers, as is the practice of relics, by which the holiness of a person is understood to endure in their mortal remains. The belief that a Christian may benefit from the grace and holiness of a saint by coming into contact with their relics promoted great veneration of relics, and the relics of the earliest martyrs were particularly prized. Perhaps that is why the head of Lucy is reputed to be at Bourges in France, while her body was taken around the Mediterranean, before coming to rest in Venice. A separated arm is believed to have been smuggled to Luitburg in Germany.

The Latin name Lucia means light, and given that Lucy's feast day is on 13 December, close to the Winter Solstice, those who reverence her came to associate her with the light of God. As her fame spread, so did the traditions attached to her feast. Like Nicholas, Lucy has become a gift-giver in Italy, with a close connection to a hot chocolate and milk dessert. In darker climes, in Scandinavia, Lucy's memory is celebrated by choosing one of the young girls in the congregation to represent her on her feast day. The chosen girl is dressed in a white robe, symbolising the saint's sanctity, with a red sash to commemorate Lucy's martyrdom. She is crowned with a wreath bearing lighted candles and leads the worship of the congregation, as they pray for God's blessing during the dark days and long nights of the winter season.

Perhaps what is so remarkable about all this is the way in which Lucy's memory is celebrated in ways far different from her roots and context in life. Her journey has not perhaps been as far as that taken by Nicholas, but it has evolved into a myriad of different forms.

Some of these traditions will seem strange, even bizarre. Others will seem rich in symbolism and faith. Perhaps the very diversity of ways in which Lucy's memory is kept alive reminds us that different things will hold a variety of meanings for different people, and strangeness is not proof of idolatry. We should seek to understand before we seek to distance ourselves. The real test of religious devotion is whether it gives rise to mere superstition or to a transforming love of God, of our neighbour and of our society, and many of the folk customs we have inherited actually have their origin in bringing people from across society together and into relationship and interdependence with one another.

The martyrdom of Lucy, and the fervent respect in which she is held, should perhaps provoke us into thinking how strong our witness is to our faith, and whether we would have the courage to endure like her if challenged. It is also a witness to the fact that a strong love for God that results in a love for humanity is an attractive witness to the love of God to humanity in Jesus Christ.

Let us pause to reflect on the strength of our witness to the love of God, and not forget to pray for those who, like Lucy, may face persecution for their faith in our own day.

God of Love, whose care for the world has inspired devotion that cannot be quenched even by the threat of death, help our faith to burn with a love for you, and bless all those who face persecution for their faith in our own day, that they may know your strength and reflect the light of your love to the world. Amen.

DAY 14
THE STAR

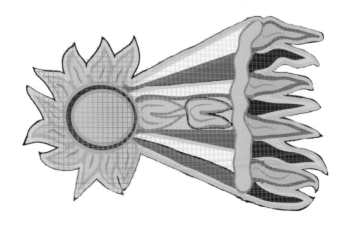

Almost every picture of the Christmas stable includes a star. However, the star and the wise men who visited Jesus after his birth aren't properly part of the Church's celebration of the Christmas story at all, but belong to the separate feast of Epiphany, usually celebrated on 6 January, after the Twelfth Night of Christmas. There are so many things that capture the imagination in the story of this visit to the infant Jesus, though, that for most of us the 'three kings who followed a star' have been folded into the Christmas story.

I

The Gospel according to Matthew tells the story. It begins with wise men (magi) arriving at the court of Herod. They have come to pay homage to the 'new-born king of the Jews' because they have observed 'the rising of his star' (Matt. 2.2). Nothing more is told to us about the star at this stage, although as the magi travel from Herod, having been directed to Bethlehem, we are told that the star reappeared and 'goes ahead of them' until it stopped over the place where 'the child' lay. We are told that they were overjoyed by the reappearance of the star.

II & III

As can be imagined, there has been much speculation about what this star was, and there are three main theories, all tied up with human beliefs about the nature of the stars.

The first draws on the suggestion that the magi might have been astrologers – astrology having been invented in ancient Babylon, and the magi having come from the East. Astrology works on the basis that the heavens reveal the future, and astrologers like to point out that occasionally there occur conjunctions of planets and stars with astrological significance. A conjunction means that, from our viewpoint on earth, the planets can appear to be in the same place and, for astrologers, this might signify the birth of a new king. In 7 BC Jupiter, the planet of Kingship, and Saturn, the planet of eternity, were conjoined in the sky, and might have been understood to signal a royal birth, but others point out that there are a number of different conjunctions that could qualify. The chief difficulty with this theory is the reappearance of the star, and the fact that it is described as moving ahead of the magi.

The second theory is that the star was in fact a comet. Comets, which were known as hairy stars in ancient times, appeared to be stars that had fallen out of their place in heaven, and were familiar to those observing the skies. Their appearance, given that those appearances were rare and sometimes unpredicted, signified upheavals in the order of human affairs, and have been seen down through human history as harbingers of doom. When Halley's Comet appeared in 1065, it was seen as prefiguring changes in the affairs of kingdoms, and was later understood as predicting the fall of the Saxon kingdom of England to the Norman invasion. I have based my picture of the star of Bethlehem on the design used for Halley's Comet on the Bayeux Tapestry, which recorded the course of the Norman invasion. We now know of course that Halley's Comet returns every seventy-six years, and did appear in 12 BC. Could this have been the star of Bethlehem? Or was it some other comet? In 1882 an unpredicted comet appeared, so bright and large that its tail covered a third of the sky and the comet was visible in daytime. Comets definitely seem to move across the sky, so meet the biblical description of movement, and can seem to point to a particular place by the angle of their tail.

There is a third theory. The life of all stars comes to an end, and occasionally a type of star called a Red Giant will use up its nuclear fuel and collapse. As it does so, it can explode in a brilliant manner – so bright that it outshines everything else in the sky. At the time of writing, there is speculation that the star Betelguese is about to undergo such a spectacular transformation, which is known as a supernova. These events cannot be predicted precisely, and scientists predict that Betelguese's transformation could become visible from earth at any moment – in the next hundred thousand years! The last supernova to be visible to the naked eye was observed by Johannes Kepler in 1604.

The seventeenth-century Anglican bishop and preacher Lancelot Andrewes once preached about the fact that Matthew speaks of 'his star' (Matt. 2.2). This was, he said, no ordinary natural event: it is Jesus' own star that rises, something new and absolutely unique, and perhaps no theory can compete with the glamour and mystery of the story as Matthew tells it.

IV

'Following a star' can become a tale of life's experiences for most of us. We can travel through life in hope towards the goals that inspire and sustain us. Perhaps the journeying in hope is almost more important than the arrival: perhaps, like T.S. Eliot's kings in his famous poem 'The Journey of the Magi', we will learn more about ourselves on the journey than by staying close in life to familiar haunts and habits.

Just as the medieval sailors navigated by the light of one star because they knew that Polaris, the North Star, always gave them a clear steer to the locations of the directions of the compass, so, for Christians, Jesus is the light of the world, a star by whom we can navigate through life. He always points us in the right direction, for in him is the fullness of life (John 1.4), and in his light we see light (Ps. 36.9). Christians believe that, like a star, God in Christ will point us in the right direction: 'whether to right or to left, you will hear a voice from behind you sounding in your ears saying, This is the way; follow it' (Isa. 30.21).

Let us reflect on the aspirations and hopes that have driven our lives, but also think of the promises in Scripture that God makes to us. By what are we guided in our own lives?

Lord God of wonder, who gave the wise men the sign of a star, by which they might navigate their journey to you; help us in life always to find in you the source of our heart's desire and, in all things, to seek out that path onto which you lead us. Amen.

DAY 15

THE MAGI

No self-respecting nativity play would be without the magi (referred to also as the three kings or wise men) who followed the star, and the story of their visit to Bethlehem. Who were these mysterious strangers and what did their visit mean?

I

Immediately after reporting Jesus' birth in a matter of one sentence, Matthew's Gospel introduces us to 'wise men' who travelled from the East following a star to lead them to the newborn King of Israel (Matt. 3). However, in the Bible there weren't three, and they weren't kings. Matthew doesn't give us a number, and later legend deduced there were three because they gave three presents – the famous gifts of gold, frankincense and myrrh. Only later were they called kings. In the Bible, the reason they are referred to as magi is because the word used is taken from Old Persian, and is the job title of the astrologers of the Persian royal court. No wonder then that they followed a star. Matthew wants to demonstrate that the birth of Jesus fulfils Scripture. Isaiah the Prophet (chapter 60) had predicted that the birth of the Messiah would be witnessed by the people of all the nations of the world, who would come to pay tribute bearing gold and frankincense. Matthew is therefore telling us that Jesus is a Messiah for everyone in the world. It may be that the magi arrived much later than the shepherds of Luke's account. When Herod wanted to intercept and kill the new-born rival for his throne, he asked the magi to tell him when exactly the star had appeared, and then instructed his soldiers to kill every child under two years of age. Had the magi already been travelling perhaps for up to two years?

II

The magi bearing their gifts quickly became a standard of Christian art. The illustration for this chapter is based upon one of the early depictions of the magi, and is taken from a mosaic in the new Basilica of St Apollinaris in Ravenna, which was decorated in the second half of the sixth century. Already the magi are three, and in order to show them as wise men from the East the Byzantine artists who made the mosaic based their figures on the most exotic Easterners they knew: the Phrygians. The magi are depicted bringing great silver basins holding their gifts, and wearing the most exuberant Eastern trousers you can imagine, as well as the famous Phrygian caps, which later became a symbol of democratic freedom in the French Revolution!

Historically, the city of Cologne in Germany invested in the three kings in a big way (not to mention St Ursula and her army of 11,000 virgins, but that's another story …). In the twelfth century, the Holy Roman Emperor Frederick Barbarossa stole the supposed relics of the three kings, which he had found in Milan, and gave them to his imperial capital. The cathedral built to house the relics took 632 years to complete, and remains the largest Gothic cathedral in the world. By then, the magi had not only become known as kings, but had been given names and coats of arms, and treated like medieval princes. The city of Cologne is dedicated to the Three Kings to this day.

III

The magi probably became referred to as kings as Christians reflected upon a particular verse in Scripture. Reflecting on the birth narrative of Matthew, they discovered another verse in Isaiah chapter 60 which seemed to be fulfilled in the story: 'nations will journey towards your light and kings to your radiance' (Isa. 60.3). What more natural than to have kings paying their respects to the newborn King of kings and Messiah of Israel?

The number three was a useful number for the kings, since in the contemporary geography textbook of Claudius Ptolemy there were three continents – Asia, Africa and Europe – and those who were very familiar with their Bibles knew also that there were three sons of Noah, from whom each of the branches of humanity were descended: Shem, Ham and Japheth. One king for each continent, and one king for each son. The whole world really did come to worship Jesus the Messiah. Even today, sometimes the kings – no longer portrayed as Persian astrologers – are shown as coming from different ethnicities of the one human family.

IV

A writer once quipped that if the magi had been wise women, they would have brought more appropriate gifts – food, warm clothing, nappies. Someone else has suggested that the gifts of the magi were the tools of their trade: gold, frankincense and myrrh may have been used in their ancient rituals and experiments. Perhaps we should accept that the magi were the equivalent of the scientists of their day. Although their science was rudimentary, they sought to understand the mysteries of creation and, in a time when all things were seen as linked, they studied the heavens to answer questions about the earth.

Perhaps one of the most extraordinary things about our universe is the existence of minds that can think, that can observe the universe and consciously develop theories about the nature of existence. Some theologians have argued that this is what is meant when Scripture says that we are made 'in the image of God', with the ability to 'fill the earth and subdue it' (Gen. 1.28). Certainly, Scripture asserts that God has given humanity a distinctive role: 'you have made him little less than a god, crowning his head with glory and honour' (Ps. 8.5). Human minds have plumbed the origins of the universe and the forces that drive the creation of galaxies and planets. We have explored the nature of life and consciousness, and unlocked many of the secrets of nature. Yet with the power of such knowledge comes great responsibility: to care for this creation, and use our knowledge in the service of wisdom.

Pause to thank God for the conscious and curious mind you have been given, and the skills and talents that it holds. Pray that you may use that knowledge and skill for the cause of good and the service of all that is lovely.

Lord of Life, as we recall the wise men who paid you humble homage after following the star to Bethlehem, teach us that in you lies the deepest truth and wisest answers to the mysteries of creation. Amen.

DAY 16
THE KING OF GOLD: MELCHIOR

The Scriptures tell us nothing about the personal details of the wise men, but of course their gifts to the newborn Christ are well known, and there is much written about the background to each gift in the Bible.

The Bible knows gold well, and throughout the Scriptures it is the most precious of metals, accorded value and respect. It is used for God and for royalty, so that the Ark of the Covenant is described as covered in gold (Heb. 9.4), and is used for all the significant furniture in the Temple of Solomon. It is the ornament of royalty, and not only are the robes of the Queen woven from cloth of gold (Ps. 45.13), but the Kings of Israel and other nations take delight in recounting the amount of gold that they have, especially since it is seen as being brought to Israel from exotic places like Ophir (1 Kings 10.22).

Yet there is also an ambivalence in Scripture towards gold. Jesus kept no money, so that he was not even able to meet his tax obligations (Matt. 17.24), and the apostles took pride in not owning any gold whatsoever (Acts 3.6).

Nevertheless, when the writer of the Book of Revelation wants to describe the heavenly city of Jerusalem, he can only express how magnificent it is by resorting to the metaphor of how golden and bejewelled it is (Rev. 21.18–21).

II

When the medieval Shrine of the Three Kings on Cologne Cathedral was opened in 1864, the remains of three men were found – one old, one middle aged, and one a youth. We may be allowed to be sceptical as to whether these might actually be the relics of the magi who visited Jesus, but it does reflect another ancient tradition in the Church – that the three kings each reflected an 'age of man': youth, maturity and old age.

In 1459 Benozzo Gozzoli was commissioned by the Medici rulers of Florence to decorate their domestic chapel with an expansive fresco of the journey of the magi. He chose to depict the three wise men in these three stages of life, and the first of the kings was represented as an old man. It is Gozzoli's picture that is used as the model for the picture of Melchior above. Tradition says that the portrait was based upon the Patriarch of Constantinople, either Joseph II or his successor, Metrophanes II, who had both recently visited the city of Florence in the hope of winning the reunion of the Eastern and Western Churches and support for the city's defence against invaders. Certainly the long flowing beard looks like that of an Orthodox hierarch.

III

Although the Bible doesn't give any names for the magi, by the beginning of the sixth century they had acquired names, so that the King of Gold became Melchior (a name which may be related to the Hebrew for 'King of Light'). By the eighth century, the Venerable Bede was describing him as old with a flowing white beard, and a whole history was invented for him not just as a Phrygian, but as a king of Persia.

His gift of gold was taken to be symbolic of the kingship that he recognised in Jesus – although symbolic meanings are not attached in the biblical story itself – emphasising again the link between gold and the nature of kingship found in the Bible. It reminds us that Jesus is hailed in Scripture as King of kings and Lord of lords. Even Jesus' disciples called him 'Lord', and the earliest simple creed of the Church of the apostles was probably quite simply: 'Jesus is Lord'.

IV

Like Melchior, Christians are called to acknowledge Jesus as the Lord of their lives, offering to him 'the gold of obedience' as the famous hymn 'O worship the Lord in the beauty of holiness' says. It reminds us of the uncomfortable thought that if this is true, then all our material wealth has to be put at the service of God, in addition to our prayers and the vocation of our lives.

Christians have always had an ambivalent attitude towards wealth. On the one hand, wealth can mean security and the ability to buy both the necessary and pleasurable things of life – what might even be described as God's blessing on our lives – but, on the other hand, Jesus himself lived in poverty, and rejected the idea that wealth and holiness belong together (Matt. 19.24). Some of the greatest saints of Christian history, like Francis, have also been the ones most ready to embrace a life of poverty, preferring spiritual riches instead. A choice falls to every Christian therefore to navigate the path between comfort and poverty.

Let us reflect on what money and wealth means to us, and how lightly or heavily we are dependent on it. Ask for God's help in understanding how our money can be used not just for our own comfort, but in the transformation of the world.

Lord God, all things come from you, and you call us to give generously of what you entrust to us. Help us to see you as the Lord of all our lives, including our wealth, so that as you were generous to us in the gift of your Son, so we may be generous in the world as a sign of your love. Amen.

THE KING OF MYRRH: BALTHASAR

Myrrh is perhaps the most enigmatic of the three gifts brought by the magi to Jesus and tradition says it is offered by Balthasar. However, like gold, it appears frequently in the Bible in ways that give clues to its possible meaning.

I

Myrrh appears in both the Old and New Testaments, where it is recognised as one of the costliest and precious substances. It is used as a perfume, mixed often with aloes, and is an ingredient in the recipe given in the Book of Exodus for the holy oil to be used to anoint and consecrate the furnishings of the Tabernacle, the sacred tent, which later evolved into the Temple at Jerusalem.

There is a specific story related in all four Gospels, where a costly pot of myrrh is used to anoint Jesus and to wash his feet. This causes some dissension among the disciples, particularly from Judas, about the waste of resources that could have been used to benefit the poor. This anointing, however, is a highly symbolic action, because of the associated uses of myrrh – a source of pain relief. At the crucifixion, Jesus is offered wine mingled with myrrh, which appears to be intended as a sedative, while myrrh appears among those spices used to anoint the dead body in preparation for burial. The story of the anointing is thus commented upon by Jesus, as an anointing in preparation for his burial, hinting at the Passion which is to come (Mark 14.8).

II

Myrrh is a gum resin, produced from the *Commiphora myrrha* tree, which grows in Arabia and parts of the Middle East. It was highly sought after, and thus traded extensively, commanding high prices. Even today it is used in medicine, and is also an ingredient (albeit in a small quantity) in a common brand of cough pastille. One theory about the gifts of the magi – contrary to a view expressed in the chapter on Melchior – is that myrrh was an extremely useful gift to give, because it was small and easily transportable, while being a ready means of exchange for goods and resources by a refugee family.

The King of Myrrh has traditionally been named as Balthasar. Bede the Venerable received a tradition that he was of African descent, but Gozzoli in his fresco depicts him as a middle-aged man of Mediterranean complexion. Gozzoli's fresco takes up three walls of the tiny Medici Chapel in the Palazzo Medici Riccardi in Florence, with one king and his entourage taking up each wall as their procession snakes around the chapel before arriving at the altar, which is set against the fourth wall. It is this picture from which I have drawn my inspiration. It is said by some to be a portrait of the Byzantine emperor John VIII Palaiologus, who was the last but one emperor of the East in a line stretching back to Constantine, the first Christian emperor. John VIII had led the delegation to Florence to try to meet with the Ecumenical Council which was meeting there at the time. He hoped to win military support against the invading Turks. The resplendent feathered crown and robes given to Balthasar by Gozzoli would be fit for a Byzantine emperor, but in the end we cannot be certain of the attribution.

III

Balthasar in legend became the King of Arabia, although the Armenians also claimed him as one of their own. Indeed, it was said by some that the kings would hold reunions at Christmas-tide in Armenia. The name in origin is actually Akkadian, the language of ancient Babylon, and means 'May Baal protect the King', Baal (the Lord) in this case being Marduk, the chief god of the Babylonians. It is therefore a strange name for a wise man considered by some to be a Christian saint! It is known in the Bible, in the Book of Daniel, as Belshazzar, the king who held a great feast, but who also viewed with alarm 'the writing on the wall', a prophecy of the downfall of his empire. Because of the name's association with the three kings, it became a relatively popular name in middle Europe.

It is the mystic meaning of myrrh, however, that has figured in the legend, since this gift of the magi may indicate that, from the very beginning, part of God's plan for Jesus would be his death upon the cross. It speaks to us of the very real connection in the person of Jesus between kingship and suffering, and that his anointing as Messiah (the Hebrew root of 'Messiah' means 'anointed') is also an anointing for his sacrificial death and burial.

IV

It is a salutary truth that faith does not bring freedom from suffering; indeed, Jesus suggested that suffering and discipleship might go hand in hand. 'Anyone who wants to be a follower of mine,' he said, 'must renounce self; he must take up his cross and follow me' (Mark 8.34). Although 'the problem of pain' – why a good God allows suffering in the world – has been a perennial issue for those wrestling with faith, there is one truth that the Christian can confidently proclaim: that God is not indifferent to our suffering, but chooses to share it with us. The birth, life and death of Jesus is an act of solidarity with humanity: God enters into our human suffering, and comes alongside all of us. The gift of myrrh is a sign that sadness and suffering is never very far away, but does not have the last word. The last word is that God is faithful and can be trusted.

Pause to reflect upon the times you have had to face suffering. How did it affect your relationship with God?

Father God, you gave us your Son that he might share in human life, its joys and its burdens. As he embraced suffering in order to win for us eternal life, grant that we may know your strength at times of our weakness, and to know that you are with us in all things. Amen.

THE KING OF FRANKINCENSE: CASPAR

The third gift was frankincense, another costly item well known to the writers of the Bible. How has this gift been understood in the Christian tradition?

I

Throughout the Bible, incense is an integral part of the worship offered to God. The five Books of Moses, at the opening of the Bible, give extensive instructions for the preparation and use of incense, and there are references to its use in the Temple at Jerusalem in many of the books of the Old Testament. Even the vision of the worship of Christ in heaven in the Book of Revelation at the very end of the New Testament speaks of the use of incense, and its symbolic meaning of representing the prayers of the faithful (Rev. 5.8, 8.4).

II

Frankincense is a particular gum resin, rather like myrrh, but has long been recognised for the beauty of its fragrance when heated. It is made from the tree whose name today is Boswellia. It is named after the eighteenth-century Scots botanist John Boswell, but it grows in mountainous regions of the Middle East, Africa and India, and has been identified for use as incense since ancient times. The name 'frankincense' actually means nothing more than 'high-quality incense', and to this day it is seen as the best and most expensive ingredient for incense, which is still widely used in the worship of several religions. This may have originally been a way to mitigate the smelliness of large unwashed crowds gathering for worship, but quickly became associated with holiness.

When Gozzoli painted his third king on the walls of the Medici Chapel, some say that he modelled the young figure upon the youthful Lorenzo de Medici the Magnificent, the future ruler of Florence, and probably the most famous member of this powerful Italian family. It doesn't quite add up though: when the original fresco was completed, Lorenzo was only ten years old, and it would have been highly unusual to use portraits of the commissioning family at the centre of such paintings. Nevertheless, the youth and vitality of this portrait makes it among the most captivating of the portraits of contemporary figures from Florentine society that grace the fresco. I have tried to capture the vitality and intensity of this unknown young man in my own picture.

III

The name assigned to the third king is Caspar, a name that proved to be even more popular in Germanic society than Balthasar, and remains popular to this day. The name derives from an ancient Chaldean word meaning 'treasurer' – the same word that is used to mean a treasurer today in contemporary Hebrew. As one of the three kings, Caspar was hailed as the King of India, as exotic and oriental location as was widely known to the classical world. One tradition even traces him to the town of Piravom in Kerala, where there is a concentration of Christian Churches dedicated to the magi. In Gozzoli's picture, Caspar is the youngest of the kings, and is perhaps a reminder that young and old are called to the worship of the King of Heaven.

The blessing that the magi brought to the Holy Family has meant that they have been seen as a source of blessing to those who remember them to this day. In some parts of Europe the Feast of the three kings is of a significance rivalling Christmas, with its own set of traditions. One of these is to record a 'visit' from the Three Kings at a home by chalking 'C+M+B' and the year's date at the entrance to a house, and asking for God's blessing on the home for the new year ahead. Not only are the three letters the initials of the kings, but they can be said to stand for the Latin tag 'Christus Mansionem Benedicat' (Christ blesses this home).

IV

In some schools of thought the three gifts are representations of the threefold office ascribed to Jesus Christ as 'Prophet (myrrh), Priest (frankincense) and King (gold)', but the link is strongest between the symbolism of frankincense and its association with holiness arising from its use in the Temple and in Christian worship. Christians believe that Jesus is the Great High Priest as argued in the fourth chapter of the Letter to the Hebrews. He is the one who comes to bridge the gap between sinful humanity and a holy God.

The holiness of Christ's presence in the world thus imparts a quality of holiness to creation, and to all aspects of human endeavour. One of the popular designs for chancel wall paintings in the medieval period was 'the Christ of the Trades', a representation of Christ standing in the midst of the tools and symbols of the artisans of the Middle Ages. Through his work as a carpenter, Christ brings blessing to all human endeavour.

The burning of frankincense in worship is also a symbol of prayer, which derives from biblical practice. As the incense ascends to heaven, so we believe that our prayers are heard before the Throne of God.

As we conclude this chapter, let us call to mind how God invited us to bring the whole of our lives before him in prayer, and how Christ invites us to holiness in everyday living.

Holy God, you gave us your Son to call us to holiness in all things. Hear our prayers, which ascend before you like incense. Grant us the grace which transforms our hearts and minds in your service, and equip us as agents for the transformation of the world. Amen.

DAY 19

HEROD

There are five kings who participate in our nativity story: after Jesus himself, and the three kings, there lurks the very worldly figure of King Herod the Great. Here, however, is a man who brings danger in his wake.

I

Herod appears in Matthew's Gospel as the King of Judaea, residing in his palace in Jerusalem. Understandably, the magi, believing that the appearance of the star heralds the birth of a new king, go first to Herod. This causes suspicions to arise in his mind, and although he directs the magi to go to Bethlehem, he is already plotting how to rid himself of a new threat to his throne. The magi avoid returning to Jerusalem, so in brutal expediency Herod orders the murder of all male children in Bethlehem under the age of two.

II

Between the Old Testament and the New, much changed in the Holy Land. By the end of the period covered by the Old Testament, the line of David no longer ruled over Israel. Instead, a series of governors and high priests held authority through a difficult period, as political fortunes in the Middle East waxed and waned. Eventually, the people of Judaea rebelled against their recently acquired Syrian masters, the Seleucid emperors, and the leader of the rebellion, Judas Maccabeus, founded a line of kings known as the Hasmoneans. The Hasmoneans fell prey in turn to the emerging Roman Empire, and the Romans installed a local mobster, Antipater from Idumea, as ruler of the area. His son was Herod, who married into the Hasmonean family, and negotiated his appointment as King of Judaea with Rome.

Historically, Herod was a huge success, rebuilding the Temple, such that he was nicknamed 'the Great', and he was the first of four Herods and one Philip from the same family to rule through the period covered by the New Testament. Herod Archelaus, his son, ruled immediately after him from Jerusalem, but was denied the crown. Another son, Herod Antipas, ruled as Tetrarch in Galilee and the surrounding district. This is the Herod who killed John the Baptist, and participated eventually in the trial of Jesus. Finally, Herod the Great's grandson, Herod Agrippa, succeeded to the throne, and it is he who sat in judgement on the Apostle Paul. None of them get a good press from the authors of the Bible.

III

The reputation of Herod the Great in history – as the consolidator of the Kingdom of Judaea, as a grandiose builder who restored the Temple and built many fine palaces and fortresses, and as a consummate politician – is a disconcerting picture for those who only know him from the pages of the Bible. What Scripture and history do agree on, though, is Herod's brutal nature; he was not averse to 'removing' members of his family who got in his way. Although there is no historical evidence for the massacre of the Innocents, the children of Bethlehem, apart from Matthew's Gospel, it nevertheless fits the depiction of the jealous and dangerous king that history records.

The picture I have offered for Herod today is based on the mosaics of the Basilica of St Mark in Venice, which were completed in the fourteenth century. They give Herod an almost pantomime appearance, dressing him in the ornate and contemporary jewelled robes of a Byzantine emperor, and putting a crown on his head that would put any court jester to shame. It is almost as if the craftsmen who created the mosaics six hundred years ago wanted to emphasise the virtually cartoon nature of his power, dependent on Roman goodwill, and given to bouts of suspicion and tyranny.

IV

I believe that Matthew, in his Gospel, has also chosen to portray a tyrant by creating a deliberate contrast between the worldly image of kingdom, which is about dominion, power and paranoia, and the Kingdom of Peace that the newborn child has come to inaugurate. At every point in his life, Jesus will avoid the panoply of greatness, emphasising that his Kingdom is one based on service and love, on sacrifice, and on the well-being and wholeness of all those who become subject to God's rule. Earthly power is, according to the Gospels, inherently unstable and unsatisfying; only the person prepared to lose their life for God's sake, who is prepared to take up their cross daily and to follow Jesus, can discover fullness of life. 'My kingdom' Jesus replied to Pilate at his trial, 'does not belong to this world' (John 18.36).

Even in our lives, we can fall into the trap of believing that if only we had more money, more control, more privilege, then we should be truly happy. However, the way of Jesus is very different – it makes a priority of loving God and loving our neighbour. The one who would find their life must be prepared to give up control, to give their life away, for – as a prayer of St Augustine says – we aim to follow Christ 'whose service is perfect freedom'.

Let us reflect on the nature of power and on the powerful, for the lesson of Scripture is that dominion seduces, but does not satisfy. How can we prioritise love in our lives?

Lord God, your son came to us as an infant, vulnerable to the schemes and desires of others. Help us to see where true life can be found, not in being served, but in serving others. Amen.

DAY 20
BETHLEHEM

For Christians, the name Bethlehem is forever linked with the birth of Christ, but why was this obscure town important, and what is its significance as the location of the birthplace of Jesus?

I

Only two Gospels – Matthew and Luke – tell the story of the birth of Jesus, but they both agree that Jesus was born in Bethlehem. For both of them, this was a matter of prophecy. For Matthew, we only discover the significance when the wise men are consulting Herod. He, in turn, consults the chief priests and scribes, and it is they who inform him that it was prophesied that the Messiah would be born in Bethlehem. They quote a prophecy from the Book of Micah, which speaks of Bethlehem as the place from which will come 'a ruler to be the shepherd of my people Israel' (Matt. 2.6).

Luke is more explicit in naming Bethlehem 'the city of David', referring back to the story in 1 Samuel chapter 16, where David is recorded as being part of the family of Jesse in the town of Bethlehem. The link with Jesus' family being descendants of David is emphasised – indeed, that is why they must travel there for the census. Later, an angel drives home the message – the long-promised Messiah has been born in the city of David.

David's city has even older references in the Bible. It was the burial place of Rachel, the wife of Jacob and, perhaps more significantly, the location of the story of Ruth. The Book of Ruth is one of only two books in the Bible named after a woman, and a non-Israelite woman at that, but she is brought into the biblical narrative because she is the grandmother of David – and therefore, for Christians, the ancestor of Jesus. She is a significant lady given that in ancient times female ancestors are rarely recorded.

II & III

After the birth narratives, the Bible falls silent about Bethlehem, but its significance was not forgotten. Justin Martyr, writing in the early second century, stresses the historicity of the story of Jesus, and recommends that doubters visit the city of Bethlehem: there, he says, you can be shown the cave that is the site of the birth of Jesus. Perhaps this was the reason that the Emperor Hadrian built a pagan temple dedicated to Adonis on top of the site shortly after AD 135. Hadrian was suppressing any form of Jewish nationalism after the last great revolt by the Jews against Roman rule, and singled out places of sacred significance for the imposition of new Roman temples: a temple of Jupiter was founded on the ruins of the Jerusalem Temple, and a temple to Venus above the site reputed to be the empty tomb of Jesus. It is this deliberate assertion of Roman religion, suppressing what had gone before, that actually provides perhaps some of the most compelling evidence of the historicity of the sites traditionally identified for these key events.

Things took a dramatic turn of fate with the conversion of the Emperor Constantine to Christianity at the beginning of the fourth century, and his sponsorship of the Church. His mother, Helena, who was already a Christian, undertook a pilgrimage to the Holy Land and set about reclaiming the sites of importance to the Christian faith. She used her son's money to fund the building of three major basilicas in the Holy Land – in Jerusalem, at the site of the empty tomb, the Church of the Resurrection, now known as the Church of the Holy Sepulchre; in Mamre, dedicated to the Holy Trinity, which refers back to a story of Abraham entertaining three angels there; and in Bethlehem, dedicated, of course, to the Nativity.

This magnificent basilica survives to this day. It has recently been restored, but shows definite signs of the ravages of many centuries, including a splendid threefold entrance which was deliberately blocked up to prevent mounted soldiers from bursting in and ransacking the place. The surviving portions of the opulent mosaics which lined the nave of the basilica can be seen in glowing splendour since the renovation, as they lead the eye to the focus of the building, which is the high altar, below which is the shrine of the Nativity. There a fourteen-point silver star, set into the floor beneath another altar, marks the very site where it is believed Mary gave birth to her son. The fourteen-pointed star, which was only introduced in the eighteenth century, bears witness to the opening of Matthew's Gospel, where he records that fourteen generations separated Jesus from the Exile, the great trauma of Israelite history, and fourteen more from David (and then fourteen more to get back to Abraham, the progenitor of Israel).

Today's picture for Bethlehem is adapted from the representation of the town in a fifth-century mosaic in the Basilica of Santa Maria Maggiore in Rome. It matches a representation of Jerusalem on the other side of the sanctuary, and the two may be modelled on the description of Jerusalem as a jewelled cubic city in the Book of Revelation. It certainly doesn't look like the mosaic of humble Nazareth! The design may, of course, recall the splendour of Helena's basilica, which would explain the line of pillars that can be glimpsed inside its entrance.

IV

To this day, Bethlehem is a fought-over town. It can easily be forgotten that Bethlehem is only five and a half miles south of Jerusalem, and in the days before the wall it was possible to walk out from the city to worship in the basilica. Emotions run deep in Bethlehem, sacred to Jews and to Christians; it is now also the home of many Muslims, and is divided from Jerusalem by the wall built by Israel in the name of protecting its citizens. Bethlehem stands at the spiritual crossroads between past and present, holiness and violence, war and peace, darkness and light.

Into such a world Jesus the Messiah was born. Perhaps we can reflect today about the sad disposition of humanity to fight over the things and places where they have emotional investment, and we can pray for peace. We can also ask: how do my actions help to bring reconciliation and contribute to the healing of the world?

O child of Bethlehem, you came to bring peace into the world. As we remember Bethlehem, a town fought over to this day, help us to be peacemakers at least in our own communities. Amen.

THE SHEPHERDS

Whereas the visitors to the newborn Jesus in Matthew's Gospel are from the elite, the wise men, in the Gospel according to Luke a completely different set of characters are described as his first followers: the shepherds. Who were they, and how do they contribute to the nativity story?

I

Luke tells us that at the same time that Jesus was being born – at night – there were shepherds out in the fields watching their sheep. To them, an unnamed angel appears announcing the birth of the Messiah. Hardly have they had time to take this in when a great heavenly choir appears, praising God in song. The shepherds agree to find the newborn child, and discover Jesus lying in a manger; they tell his parents how the angelic message had been brought to them. Then, we are told, they went on their way rejoicing and praising God.

II

The fact that the shepherds were in their fields has been seen as a token that Jesus must have been born at a time other than mid-winter, since flocks may have been penned – or even housed indoors – for the winter months, although the evidence is not conclusive.

Shepherds, those who did the humdrum shift work in looking after flocks, had very little status in the ancient world, and so Luke describes visitors from a very different demographic when compared to Matthew. These are humble folk, and they reflect the earliest constituencies to which the teaching of Jesus appealed. Jesus compared himself to a shepherd in his teaching, and drew on analogies from shepherding life, speaking of the lost sheep, and of the judgement of God at the end of time in shepherding terms. Indeed, the majority of Jesus' ministry seems to have been oriented towards the poorest and most sidelined people of society. It is sometimes argued that Jesus used parables drawn from farming life in order to be understood by those who came to listen to his teaching, but it is quite clear that the parables were sometimes deliberate in their mysteriousness (Matt. 13.10). What is clear is that farming and peasant society was familiar to Jesus; it is where he lived his life, and in doing so demonstrated God's bias towards the poor.

The song of the angels – 'Glory to God in the highest, and on earth peace, good will to all' – quickly made it into Christian worship and hymnody. One of the greatest and oldest of all Christian hymns is the 'Gloria in Excelsis', which begins with the message of the angels, and then elaborates on the praise of God. It is found in worship manuals of the third and fourth centuries, and very early on became incorporated into liturgies of morning prayer. From there it became part of the standard text in the Eucharistic liturgy, and is regarded as one of the central texts used in Christian worship, with settings by very many of the great composers.

III

Despite interest in the story of the shepherds, tradition and legend never got around to giving backstories to the shepherds in the way in which the wise men were invested with consistent names, histories and tokens of nobility. From the very beginning, their ordinariness became their hallmark, and they retained their anonymity, except in individual texts or contexts.

They were, however, regarded as much more accessible to ordinary folk, and quickly became characters in the medieval mystery plays, where the story of the Nativity was played out. Whereas the three kings retained a serious quality, the shepherds developed in a down-to-earth style, becoming figures of humour and slapstick comedy. In the Wakefield cycle of mystery plays, for example, Coll the shepherd boy complains about life, the weather, and snobbish gentry, while Gib, a second shepherd, speaks at length about the perils of marriage, and medieval sex lives. The characters of the shepherds were also used to introduce musical interludes in the plays, and therefore pictures of them from this period often include musical instruments like bagpipes and recorders, with which the shepherds were understood to while away their time stationed in the fields.

The picture that I have adapted in this chapter is taken from the Copenhagen Psalter, a twelfth-century English manuscript that became a prized possession of the Danish royal family. In addition to the Book of Psalms, the Psalter contains meditations on the life of Christ, and even an alphabet, which suggests that it was used in the royal household as a teaching aid. The picture of the angel appearing to the shepherds is a fairly conventional image, with the words spoken by the angel reproduced as a scroll held in his hand on which the message is inscribed. It is notable, however, that the shepherds are portrayed with rough features and a rustic quality. Their peasant background remains an enduring feature.

IV

It is a reminder to us that we find God's favour not because of our great qualities, our intelligence, beauty or nobility, but simply because God delights in us as he has made us. Christianity is not a religion in which we try to score points in order to be worthy of God's love, but rather based upon God's gracious attitude towards us: 'This is what love really is: not that we have loved God, but that he loved us and sent his Son as a sacrifice to atone for our sins' is a key message in one of the short letters in the Bible that are ascribed to the Apostle John (1 John 4.10). Jesus himself found his home among the ordinary, and often sought out friendship and hospitality from those that society would otherwise have frowned upon – people like the tax collector Zacchaeus, the fishermen who became his first disciples, and the two unmarried women, Mary and Martha, who made a home with their brother, Lazarus.

Let us reflect on God's delight for us as we are, and the good news that greets us in Christ. For we are called in the simplicity of our being to listen to the message of the angels, and turn aside to worship him.

Lord Jesus Christ, whose birth was shared with the shepherds through the message of an angel, and the singing of the angelic choirs, help us to praise you, not only with our lips but in our lives. Amen.

DAY 22
THE OX & THE ASS

The ox and the ass are familiar figures in the crib set accompanying the infant Jesus, but what exactly was the 'stable' where Jesus was born, and who were his companions there?

I

Matthew says nothing about where Jesus was born, apart from naming Bethlehem. Luke, however, is much more specific. It is Luke who specifies that Jesus was born in Bethlehem during a census, which, according to him, required all the descendants of David to return to the town. When the baby was born, Luke writes, his mother 'wrapped him in swaddling clothes', and 'laid him in a manger, because there was no room for them at the inn' (Luke 2.7). The use of the manger is repeated no less than three times – in the original description, again in the message of the angel, and again when the shepherds actually arrive. We are told that this is where the shepherds found the infant – lying in a manger. This has been understood to mean that Jesus was born in a stable, although no further details are added, and there is no mention of the presence of any animals.

II

There has been great discussion by theologians about what the presence of the manger might imply. Traditionally, this has been received by the Church as Jesus being born in a stable, and artists down through the centuries have been happy to illustrate exactly that. However, recent analysis of the text has reflected on the words used. The word for 'inn' in the original Greek text means something more like a 'guestroom' than a 'hotel'. It is the same word as used for the 'upper room' in which Jesus held the Last Supper. If this was the case, then it reflects the design of many smaller houses in Palestine in New Testament times, where the household animals were brought in at winter to the downstairs area, while the family lived upstairs – with the heat of the animals downstairs providing, I suppose, an early form of central heating!

In these circumstances, Joseph and Mary should be seen as seeking out their relatives in Bethlehem, but because there were so many guests, there was no room for them in 'the family room', and they had to move into the downstairs room, usually reserved for animals, complete with 'manger'.

This might actually fit with tradition, in which, as we have discovered, it is actually a cave that is identified as the birthplace of Jesus. It is entirely possible that the cave served as a sort of cellar for the family home on top of it, but with the cave normally being reserved for the use of animals.

III

So where do the ox and the ass come from? As the ancient Christian theologians read their Bibles, they were keen to cross-reference the work of God. The entire Old Testament was seen as preparing for the divine revelation of God's love in Christ. The story of Jesus' life could therefore be predicted in enormous detail by reference to Old Testament prophecy. As scholars combed the Scriptures, two in particular stood out.

In the book of the prophet Habakkuk, there is an obscure verse, the Hebrew of which is unclear. It is usually translated as 'Through all generations you have made yourself known' (Hab. 3.2). However, Greek was the language of the early Church, and a Greek translation of the Old Testament called the Septuagint (after the seventy translators who worked on it) was the text most commonly referred to. There, the verse (in English translation) reads something like: 'In the middle of two living creatures you shall be known'. The living creatures are even more obscure, but then there is the verse in Isaiah. Isaiah 1.3 reads: 'An ox knows its owner, and a donkey its master's stall; but Israel lacks all knowledge, my people has no discernment.' For the theologians of ancient times this was 'game, set and match'. Clearly, when Jesus was born, he was laid in a manger, and was recognised as master by an ox and an ass, two living creatures, between whom he was laid.

Very quickly icons of the Nativity took up the theme, the ox and the ass becoming ubiquitous in the Orthodox tradition, where the image was theologised even more – the ox (a clean animal in Leviticus) clearly represented the Jewish people and the ass (an unclean animal) the nations not chosen by God – yet Jesus came as Saviour to both. This is just a taste of a way of reading Scripture that was once quite common, but quite different to the literal and plain reading preferred today.

This tradition passed into Western painting, and I have reproduced my version of the ox and the ass from a painting by Domenico Ghirlandaio of the nativity scene, in which the ox and the ass are depicted as waiting for the infant Christ to be placed by his mother into the crib.

IV

For animal lovers, all the theology may be swept aside. It is just fitting that the animals were the first to be on hand to greet the Saviour of the world. Yet there is a serious theological point here. Even if we do not read the Scriptures in a symbolic way, the presence of the ox and the ass is a reminder of the physicality of the birth of Jesus, and the universal dimensions of his incarnation. For Jesus comes to us as Lord of all creation, and as 'even the winds and waves obey him', so also the animal world is part of God's good creation, and caught up in the pattern of redemption. 'The created universe is waiting with eager expectation', wrote St Paul (Rom. 8.19), and although there is nothing in the Bible to suggest that there will be animals – or pets – in heaven, a holistic view of God's work means that animals and the natural world are sacred also.

Let us pause and think of the beauty of all creation, of the way in which God speaks to us through seasons and weather, through plant and animal life.

Creator God, you are the Lord of all creation. Give us a healthy respect for all that your hand has made, and teach us to be good stewards of all the earth. Amen.

DAY 23

THE LITTLE DRUMMER BOY

Our nativity scene is getting crowded now. The members of the Holy Family, the saints and angels, the animals, the shepherds and the wise men have all arrived to offer their homage. But wait, who is that in the corner crying? It appears to be a little drummer boy.

I

The wise men must be allowed their entourage, of course, but there is no mention of a little drummer boy among them in Scripture. However, while this particular character in the nativity story is a newcomer, music already appears in the Nativity story with the song of the angels. This, with the story of the drummer boy, who was left behind by the magi, can draw our attention to the importance that the Bible places on music in the worship of God.

Music, the talent of the human being to weave the sounds of an instrument or voice into a form of beauty expressed by harmony, pattern or rhythm, is deeply evocative of human emotions and of our deepest spiritual impulses.

Music has been used in divine worship for as long as human memory can tell. Miriam, the sister of Moses, we are told, sang a song at the deliverance of Israel at the Red Sea; David, we have learned, was an expert at the harp and in song, with many of the psalms in the Book of Psalms attributed to him. We have been introduced to at least two of the three canticles that Luke incorporates into his birth narrative. From Isaiah's vision of heaven, in chapter 6 of his prophecy, through to the Book of Revelation, with its frequent references to worship in heaven, song is a vital component in the praise of the Most High.

II

Christian engagement with the story of Christmas has been augmented by a lively imagination and a vast hinterland of legend. Although he is a relative newcomer to the stable, the little drummer boy has nevertheless secured his place in people's affections. He appears originally in a song written in 1941 by Katherine Kennicott Davis, an American songwriter. This song was made popular when it was first issued as a recording in 1951 by the Trapp Family Singers, who themselves were later popularised in the film *The Sound of Music*, and the song featured at the top of the Christmas music charts in a number of different versions for many years afterwards. Today 'The Little Drummer Boy' has joined the list of favourite Christmas carols.

The song draws on an old and pleasing Czech story. After the wise men had visited, it recounts, they left their gifts and departed. Only then do Mary and Joseph become aware of a small figure crying in the corner of the stable. It is a little drummer boy, part of the entourage, who has been left behind. Mary invites him to play for the infant Jesus, who rewards him with a smile. For some, this may be pure schmaltz. For others, the most humble of gifts sincerely given are part of what makes Christmas truly Christmas.

III

For centuries, the celebration of Christmas has been accompanied by the singing of carols. The oldest carol for which we have a record is 'Come, Redeemer of the Nations', written in Latin in the fourth century by the Church father Ambrose. Originally, the word 'carol' referred to any seasonal song, and there were Easter and Pentecost carols, as well as carols for Christmas. Gradually, though, the tradition of carolling at Easter and other times faded, while carols at Christmas became an indispensable feature of the feast.

In a carol, songwriters could give free rein to their devotion. Some carols from earlier times stressed the Christmas narrative ('The First Nowell'), others addressed doctrinal questions in a more oblique manner ('O Come All Ye Faithful'). Some were rich in symbolism ('The Holly and the Ivy', 'I Saw Three Ships'), and yet others told stories that are frankly bizarre ('The Cherry Tree Carol', which has the infant Christ from inside the womb performing a miracle for his hungry mother when Joseph is uncharacteristically uncharitable). Later carols began as works of poetry ('In the Bleak Midwinter') and others from the legends of popular saints ('Good King Wenceslas'). 'The Little Drummer Boy' takes its place in this rich tradition.

IV

We have already noted the distinctive human ability to probe and measure the rules of creation in science, but alongside the sciences recognition also needs to be given to the arts. For if science aids us in understanding the natural world, then the arts give us insight into the world of emotion, and of human spirituality.

One of the benefits of a faith in God is a sense of the source of these remarkable human abilities to plumb the depths of the world, and to organise sound or colour or shape to create something meaningful and new. There is someone to be grateful to for these gifts.

One of the words coined by the Reformation theologian Philip Melanchthon was 'synergy', a word he used to indicate the way in which the human soul could resonate and work with God in the healing and salvation of humanity and nature. It is perhaps a word that we as people of faith could also use for the creative process. God invites us to use our minds, our imaginations and our senses, to build on the world of nature, and create new things that speak of beauty, meaning or mystery.

My wife is a musician, and she never fails to amaze me with her ability to stir emotion by the power of music, while one of the pleasures of writing this book has been to explore the limits of my ability with art, and to create new (and humble) versions of old masterpieces to accompany the text.

Let us pause to reflect on the wonderful ability of humanity to enrich creation through the arts, and let us thank God for whatever gifts of self-expression or talent that he has given to us by way of hobby, craft or industry.

Lord God, you spoke and all things came into being. We thank you for the creativity that you have given to humanity to echo your creation in the production of works of art and beauty. Help us to see what we each can create with the talents you have placed in our hearts. Amen.

MARY MOTHER OF GOD

We have arrived at Christmas Eve, the night of Jesus' birth, and we return to the very human figure with which we began – Mary, the mother of Our Lord.

I

Mary remains at the heart of the early chapters of the Gospels of Matthew and Luke: it is her consent to become the mother of Our Lord that makes the story of salvation possible, and her courage and endurance that brings the birth of Jesus to fruition. However, these bold decisions are also the fruit of God's grace at work in her life: we cannot draw a line between where the work of the human begins and the divine ends. The actual birth of Jesus is accomplished without much discussion in the Bible, but Mary immediately cares for her baby as any mother would – preparing swaddling clothes and wrapping Jesus in them. Swaddling clothes are often better known as 'swaddling bands' in many versions of the Bible. These items of clothing bound babies tightly to stop them moving their limbs, thus keeping a baby safe and soothing it. They were much valued in antiquity and in the medieval period, but fell out of favour in the seventeenth century. To be unswaddled was to be uncared for, so the evangelist is telling us that Jesus is given the best of motherly care.

Beyond the birth narratives, Mary does not feature often in the story of Jesus' life as recorded in the Gospels. When she does, it is always in the role of someone who cares deeply for her son and what happens to him: speaking of her worry when Jesus is lost in the Temple as a twelve-year-old, concerned for the success of a marriage feast at Cana, or at the way in which Jesus' reputation might be damaged by misunderstanding. She is there at the foot of the cross. Mary therefore is presented as the archetype of motherhood.

However, she is also the person of faith. Her 'yes' to God sets the birth narrative going, and at its close Luke tells us that 'Mary treasured up all these things and pondered over them' (Luke 2.19). It fits the tradition that Luke got his stories from Mary herself, but it also speaks of a person who reflects and prays, and understands the significance of what is happening.

II & III

The picture I offer today is perhaps second only to the crucifixion in the iconography of Christian faith. Known as a

Madonna (simply the Italian for 'My Lady') and child, it shows the infant Jesus in the arms of his mother. It is an image that has been reproduced countless times and in very different forms. It is the subject matter of some of the most famous icons of history, and the most varied. This particular image is adapted from a Madonna by Antoniazzo Romano, an Italian artist of the fifteenth century, and seems to pick up on the intimacy between mother and child, as Jesus tugs on his mother's robes to attract her attention. It brings to life that very human story that interacts with the divine at the heart of Christianity.

Mary became prominent in the history of Christian doctrine, not in her own right at first, but because of her pivotal role in the life of Jesus. Her physicality and identity underscored and affirmed his physicality and identity. As the tides of controversy ebbed and flowed in the early centuries of Christianity, and thinkers and theologians sought to understand the action of God in Christ, the story of Mary prevented Jesus from becoming some disembodied manifestation of God. The incarnation is real.

From the third century, a new title for Mary started to be used. She was called the 'God Bearer', or the 'Mother of God', because she had carried in her womb the presence of God himself incarnate. At the Council of Ephesus, recognised by the Church as the Third Ecumenical Council, in AD 431, Mary was awarded this title formally, and it is a title commonly used for Mary in the Orthodox Church to this day, although more rare in Western Christianity. It underscores the central claim of Christianity that 'in him [Jesus] God in all his fullness chose to dwell' (Col. 1.19). Mary's role is to underline who Jesus is – she guarantees his humanity by her humanity, and as the Mother of God, she is also witness to his divinity.

IV

Mary has become a popular focus of Christian devotion. Some say that she brings an element of the feminine into the centre of a Christian faith in which there is an excess of masculinity. However, Mary inevitably leads us to her son, while also inviting us to meditate upon that most important of Christian virtues: tenderness. Tenderness is a form of love, but it is love that is offered gently, quietly, and without looking for recompense. Tenderness is a form of care that solicits response, not by struggle but by grace, gently coaxing the beloved into fullness of life. It is fitting that the loving bond between a mother and a child should therefore be at the heart of the story of Christmas.

As we stand on the verge of the Feast of the Nativity, let us give thanks for this historical family that opens the way for God to enter the world. Let us be thankful for the courage of Mary in her embrace of God's will, and for the solace and protection offered by Joseph. Let us recognise the hand of God's providence in working through the history of Israel, through Ruth of Bethlehem and through David, through John, Zechariah and Elizabeth, Anna and Joachim, in a very human drama to bring about the revelation of his love.

As we stand on the threshold of Christmas, let us pause and recall that through this one human family the culmination of the history of God's people, and God's promises, are for Christians brought to fulfilment.

Lord God, you have acted in the lives of prophets and of saints to reveal your love to the world. As we remember this very human family, and especially Mary, Mother of God, through whom your love was brought in a new way into this world, bless us and our homes, that love and peace may abound. Amen.

DAY 25
THE CHRIST CHILD

We come at last to the Feast of the Nativity, and we ourselves draw near to the stable so that we might be introduced to the Christ child.

I

Matthew and Luke give a fairly extensive narrative for the period leading up to the birth of Jesus, both taking two chapters of their respective Gospels to tell distinctive but complementary stories. The Gospel according to Mark skips the story of Jesus' birth entirely and hurries on to the ministry of

John the Baptist, who erupts into Judaea's life with a message of repentance, and to whom Jesus comes for baptism.

John starts from a different place entirely. His Gospel begins from the vantage point of eternity, starting from the time before creation itself, and pondering on the very nature of the divine. From the fathomless depths of God's being and from eternity God is manifested as the Word, bringing creation into being, and as the source of life and light. One can almost sense his amazement as he speaks of this light coming into the world, heralded by John the Baptist, and the light drawing humanity into relationship. There are only two characters in the prologue of John's Gospel – John the Baptist and the Word.

Christians speak of the mystery of the incarnation, the way in which God himself assumed human flesh, and St John the Evangelist is a key witness in his prologue: 'The Word became flesh', he writes, 'he made his home among us, and we saw his glory, such glory as befits the Father's only Son, full of grace and truth' (John 1.14).

II

It might be said that the enormity of God's action in Christ Jesus was of such proportions that it took human theologians four hundred years to articulate it. But this would be untrue, for the mystery of the incarnation goes beyond *any* articulation. What we can say is that the disciples perceived in the person of their Master an experience of God so profound that they could acknowledge Jesus as 'My Lord and my God!' (John 20.28). For the person of faith, it is a straight line from the birth narratives of Jesus to the declarations on the nature of God and Christ in the Nicene Constantinopolitan Creed, which is the basis for Christian orthodoxy (the right praise of God) to this day. In being introduced to the infant Christ, we believe that we are in the presence of the Word of God, of God himself acting to bring salvation to the world, for 'God was in Christ reconciling the world to himself' (2 Cor. 5.19).

The second commandment imposed a ban on any image of God, and yet Christians believe that the image of God has been revealed to us in Jesus Christ. 'He is the image of the invisible God' (Col. 1.15). Therefore, apart from two periods of Christian history when images were seen as dangerous temptations to idolatry (the Iconoclastic crisis in the East in the fifth century, and the Reformation in the West in the sixteenth), Christians have felt able to delineate pictures of Christ and the saints. The image I have chosen for today is adapted from a painting of the Madonna and Child done by Fra Giovanni de Fiesole, who was also known as Fra Angelico (The Angelic Friar) because of his sublime skills as an artist. It shows the Christ child, who sits with Our Lady, but with all the gravity of the King of Heaven and Earth – indeed, in some icons Christ is shown reigning as King, even when a child – in extreme cases, even reigning thus from the womb. Indeed, Christ's halo is unique: even in infancy it bears the mark of the cross and the atoning sacrifice to which his life is oriented.

III

We have already noted the way in which other gospels were composed in the early centuries of Christianity which emphasised the miraculous, but which by and large failed to meet the test of being received by the Church as having been written by an apostle, or the companion of an apostle. These apocryphal gospels often set out extremely detailed accounts of the Nativity, and several references have already been made to the Proto-evangelium (or early gospel) of James. While elements of such legendary material have occasionally been incorporated in the

Christmas story, by and large they are no more than legendary accounts. There is one episode in the apocryphal Gospel of James, however, that always catches my attention.

Joseph leaves Mary (interestingly in the protection of his other sons) while she is giving birth to seek the aid of a midwife. As Christ is born, in the middle of the night, something strange happens. Time itself stops. The stars stop moving, the birds hang still in mid-air, people eating are frozen in the middle of lifting food to their mouths. As Christ is born, the universe itself stops to mark this most significant of events.

IV

Many years ago, in school, I was given the assignment of deciding which was the more important feast, Easter or Christmas. I unhesitatingly chose Easter, for its close connection with the atonement wrought on the cross, and the vindication of Christ's victory over sin and death represented by his rising from the dead. While I hold on to that, I am now inclined to favour Christmas, for this is the moment when the universe changed, when, as the great theologian Athanasius put it, 'God became man that man might become God'. In the celebration of the Nativity, we celebrate the moment when God joined his nature to his creation, becoming one of us, that we might become the bearers of eternal life.

In the Gospel according to Matthew, when Joseph is advised to hold fast and to marry Mary, he is referred to the prophecy of Isaiah: 'A young woman is with child, and she will give birth to a son and call him Immanuel' (Isa. 7.14). Strangely, though, there is no account of Jesus being named thus by Joseph or Mary. It is, none the less, the most significant of names, because it means 'God is in our midst'.

This is the point to which our journey towards Christmas brings us – to the realisation that the Christ child is God in our midst, and 'If God is on our side, who is against us?' (Rom. 8.31).

Happy Christmas. For a prayer today, here is the final verse of one of the best-loved Christmas carols.

O Holy Child of Bethlehem, descend to us, we pray,
Cast out our sin, and enter in; be born in us today.
We hear the Christmas angels their great glad tidings tell,
O come to us, be born in us, Our Lord Immanuel.